Praise

"On my personal quest for healing I've found that ... ... key! In *Heart Healing: The Power of Forgiveness to Heal a Broken Heart*, Susyn Reeve shares her personal heart break and the path she followed to be a mighty expression of Love in the world. This book serves as your personal heart healing coach to heal the pain of a current heart break and to, more importantly, free your heart and mind of the wounds of the past. Don't wait, say, Yes, to healing your heart today.
—Jamie Lynn Sigler, actress on *The Sopranos*

"In her new book, *Heart Healing: The Power of Forgiveness to Heal a Broken Heart*, Susyn Reeve answers the question, 'Is it really possible to free your heart and mind of the emotional wounds of the past?' Not only is her answer a resounding YES—but she provides the inspiration, information, and easy to apply guidance and practices to heal your heart from heartbreak. She knows the territory and invites you to step fully into your own heart healing journey."
—G. Brian Benson, author of *Habits for Success: Inspired Ideas to Help You Soar*

"Heartbreak is a painful fact of life. Be prepared to free your heart, because you were born worthy. Read *Heart Healing: The Power of Forgiveness to Heal a Broken Heart* and learn how to live and Love."
—Nell Merlino, creator of Take Our Daughters to Work Day and Born Worthy

"Susyn Reeve has been my life coach for the past two years. She's made a powerful difference in my life. Her coaching goes far beyond being supportive. She possesses the ability to shine light on the crux of my issues, and gently but firmly leads me to my own insights with her eloquent wisdom and willingness

to share her heart so generously. Heart healing is in store for you when you read this book!"
—Dottie Coakley, author of *Chattanooga Girl*

"Having your heart break, no matter what the circumstance, is an excruciatingly painful experience. Because we are human beings and don't always act in a loving way, we will all get our heart broken at some time in our lives. It takes courage to experience heartbreak in a way that leads to healing. We often think that if we let enough time go by and don't think of it, the pain will go away. Unfortunately, although that may eventually happen, it is not the process that allows us to live our lives fully, joyfully, and peacefully.
When we have the fearlessness to face our heartbreak and recognize the lessons it holds for us, we can transform an ugly experience into a lifechanging, positive one. Susyn's book gives us the map for a more fulfilling, heart-healing journey. When we have the courage to take the steps, read the messages, and do the exercises, we CAN come out on the other side a better, happier, more loving person."
—Calla M. Crafts, Senior Consulting Partner, the Ken
   Blanchard Companies

"Not forgiving someone else—or yourself—is like carrying around a twenty-five-pound sack of potatoes. It's uncomfortable, it's a burden, and it drags you down. But forgiving is not an easy task. That is why you need *Heart Healing*. It is filled with inspiring ideas on how you can empty that sack-of-unforgiving so that you can lead a richer, fuller, and happier life."
—Allen Klein, author of *You Can't Ruin My Day* and *The Healing Power of Humor*

"*Heart Healing: The Power of Forgiveness to Heal a Broken Heart* is a compassionate and immensely helpful guide to get through one of the toughest experiences that happens to us—a broken heart. The forgiveness required for healing is almost impossible, it seems. But with the clear guidance and personal approach in this book, Susyn Reeve leads us through with the kindness of a best friend, and the wisdom we all need from those who can navigate this landscape with authority. Reeve helps us with lovingkindness to explore what we ourselves may be too afraid to see, in detail when and where we need it."

—Colin Harrington, The Bookstore, Lenox, MA

"Susyn Reeve is an amazing champion of finding ways to heal one's heart. With experience fostered by paying attention to her own challenges and working at devising ways for others to read their own signs of hurt, Susyn brings new awareness of reconnecting with one's own love within. In this book, you will find answers on how to heal yourself. We are proud to have Susyn in our Hamptons community. BRAVO, SUSYN!"

—Eva Growney, architect and founder of Ensouled Hearts™

"Susyn Reeve's *Heart Healing: The Power of Forgiveness to Heal a Broken Heart* is filled with 'aha' moments that will help heal any reader who has experienced acute emotional pain. This book is direct and honest. Reeve doesn't shy away from life's hard truths, but she has the experience and wisdom to offer practical advice on how to cope through heartbreak and ultimately thrive. Her story will resonate with readers, showing them their experiences are valid and their pain can be overcome."

—Kate Allan "The Latest Kate," author of *You Can Do All Things*

"If you're plagued by a broken heart, filled with unresolved anger, grief, frustration, and disappointment, Susyn has laid out the formula for the greatest healer of all…forgiveness. This book will help to heal your wounds and give you the tools to step into your own power. And if you want to make a positive difference in this world, it's essential to do this work."

—Sharla Jacobs, CEO, Thrive Academy, author of *The Art of Attracting Clients*

"This is the book we need now. As the world polarizes around race, religion, gender, and nationalism, Susyn Reeve's *Heart Healing* offers an honest and comprehensive blueprint for breaking free of the hurt spiral."
—Morgana Rae, www.morganarae.com, author of *Financial Alchemy*

"Susyn Reeve's latest work may be the most important read we'll ever dive into. *Heart Healing* illuminates the hidden judgements that run our actions. The power of this book lies in proven practices to free ourselves to live in tandem with our deepest power. Bravo, Susyn, and thank you!"
—Ryan Weiss, life coach and creator of www.WakingUpWithRyan.com

"If ever there was a time to dive deeply into forgiveness, it's now, today, this moment—this moment, when waves of "us vs. them" are raising their ugly heads once more, calling us to step away from building community and honoring diversity and back into competition and winning at all cost. How did we get here? In *Heart Healing*, Susyn Reeve helps us see that the real struggle and the first solution is within. With loving hands and a wise heart, Susyn invites us to heal our wounded hearts as we move through her gentle processes to forgive ourselves, our family, body, and relationships. Want to make a difference in the world? Start here."
—Janet Conner, author *of Soul Vows* and *Find Your Soul's Purpose*

"I love Susyn's writing! Her new book, *Heart Healing*, touched my heart and opened my mind to forgive and let go of the emotional wounds that had kept me stuck for much too long. I'll be reading and using this book over and over again, and of course, recommending it to everyone I know."
—Elissa Goodman, Holistic Nutritionist and author of *Cancer Hacks*

"Every positive change or dream begins with a change of heart. In her powerful new book, *Heart Healing*, Susyn unveils the key role forgiveness plays in healing the past—so we can bring the aliveness of an open heart to every facet of living.

Beyond the inspiration, which really did speak directly to something in me that had me nodding my head, I especially appreciate the many practical exercises for applying heart healing to my specific challenges and growth. The organization of the book made it easy to go directly to those areas in which I want to invite healing. For those who sense that heartbreak, old pain, and resentments are holding them back from the flow of love, joy, and peace they're ready for—this book is the perfect doorway to *Heart Healing*."
—Rikk Hansen, America's "Calling" Coach and Creator of
  www.BrilliantNext.com

"A broken heart is so hard to heal, and often it takes years or even a lifetime to put the shattered pieces back together. *Heart Healing* is a guide that can help the heartbroken pick up the scattered fragments of their hearts and piece them back together, as well as a beautiful and encouraging read for anyone who has ever felt the sting of a broken heart."
—Misty Griffin, author of *Tears of the Silenced*

"I've known Susyn for over thirty years. I appreciate her ability to thoroughly research her topic from both her personal experiences and from many other experts. She has successfully brought structure to support anyone healing their heart, which is every one of us. She uses great examples and gives us a focus to assist all of us to be the best self we can be."
—Shanti Gilbert, MSW, PD, MS

"Who hasn't been heartbroken? Who hasn't cried themselves to sleep after being dumped? Who hasn't been enraged at being ill-treated and disrespected? Most, if not all, of us have been there. Heartbreak is the potential outcome we want to suppress and forget about when we open our one and only tender heart and become vulnerable to another human; when we love. What makes Susyn Reeve's approach to the topic so different is that she asks us to welcome all the messiness, the tears, and the strong emotions, and our hidden shadows, imps, and monsters, not to a pity party but to a life-affirming bash from which we are certain to emerge stronger, happier, wiser, and crazily enough, more open and trusting. Let Susyn's gift for working emotions through to that happy ending you were hoping for guide you through the process. Don't turn inward without guidance and nurse your rage, grief, and loss. Turn to this book and grow. You have the choice."

—Hilary V. O'Donnell, author of *Naxos: An Unexpected Life on a Greek Island*

"It's one thing to know the importance of doing forgiveness work; it's another thing entirely to know how to forgive in order to heal a broken heart. In *Heart Healing*, Susyn delivers an inspiring and pragmatic how-to guide for walking the tumultuous path of heartbreak with courage, so that you can ultimately forgive, heal and enjoy life again, even more fully."

—Megan Walrod, Business & Life Coach at www.MeganWalrod.com

HEART
HEALING

Heart Healing: The Power of Forgiveness to Heal a Broken Heart

Library of Congress Cataloging
ISBN: (p) 978-1-63353-588-6, (e) 978-1-63353-589-3
Library of Congress Control Number: 2018952273
BISAC—SEL033000—SELF-HELP / Self-Management / Anger Management

Printed in the United States of America.

HEART HEALING

The Power of Forgiveness to Heal a Broken Heart

SUSYN REEVE

Mango Publishing

CORAL GABLES, FL

To the wisdom of my heart:
Thank you for speaking loud enough for me to hear
and clear enough for me to understand.

CONTENTS

PART III: PRACTICING FORGIVENESS

FOREWORD

There's no pain quite like that of a broken heart. The depths of agony, loss, and confusion knock us off our joy with darkness we only know when we are under its weight. We swear that we will never let ourselves be that vulnerable again…enough is enough.

When our hearts are broken, we question everything: "Will I ever be truly loved? What is wrong with me? How dare he do this to me! Why am I still crying?" It feels as though our pain may never subside.

While a broken heart is utter torture, in its depth also lives the opportunity for miraculous transformation if we allow ourselves to walk the journey from suffering to healing. It may be hard to hear this right now, as healing may feel so far away, if even possible at all. The toughest journeys are best walked with a guide. And you, love, are in good hands, my Godmother's hands.

There are few moments when *life* offers us an earth angel—someone who interrupts our journey as if to say, "Hello, we are meant to meet, and your life will forever change now that I'm in it." I was twenty-six years old and Susyn was sixty-two when I asked her to be my Godmother as we sat on the floor of a new friend's apartment. We'd met only hours earlier.

Just months before this miraculous encounter, I'd had a massive "aha" experience and took a hard right turn from the life I'd planned into the daunting but thrilling world of the unknown. I'd recently come to understand how my ego had been informing the actions that were directing my path and had begun the journey of surrendering to life's plan for me.

I needed someone to guide me. And *life* gave me the perfect person.

It's been seven years, and Susyn has guided me through two *major* break-ups that left me shattered and raw.

She listens, honors, and is present to my pain, asks me questions, and offers her experience. She supports my wins and loves me through my losses.

Susyn is a gifted storyteller. She heals through her stories. Whenever I've turned to her in a moment of pain or worry, Susyn answers with a story, a story that shares a time when she experienced the kind of agony I am currently mixed up in. Every time, her personal story has given me perspective. Each story offered me an opportunity to see my situation as something that is moving and changing, as opposed to something painfully fixed and stuck.

Susyn shares her stories of heartbreak, forgiveness, and healing in *Heart Healing: The Power of Forgiveness to Heal a Broken Heart*.

Most importantly, each step of the way, Susyn offers you a tool—a technique she has honed over her expansive career. The gold of *Heart Healing* lies in putting what Susyn provides into practice.

The heartbreak and depression that can set in feel so isolating, like we are all alone in our suffering and no one can understand the depth of our pain. Susyn writes about the torment that has happened in her head when heartbreak tore her apart. You will read her words with a familiar nod. She gets it; she really gets it. And then she delivers us to the healing waiting for us.

As much as we may try to avoid pain and play it safe, life will break our hearts. It's inevitable. After the heartbreak, we too often sit in the suffering caused by our judgments of our exes and ourselves. We contemplate the many ways we messed up…the things we wished we had said, and the things we wished we had never said. We stew in our self-torment.

That darkness is overwhelming, so we value finding closure. Typically, when we say "closure," we mean, "How quickly can I get over this? How can I stop feeling the pain and just get on with my life?" The gift Susyn offers in *Heart Healing* is a more radical, powerful approach to overcoming heartbreak. Rather than seeking closure by closing our hearts, Susyn teaches us to keep our hearts open. She grounds us in our vulnerability in order to feel it all—to move through and process what needs to be examined if we are to heal truly. On the other side of our heartbreak is our healing, if we engage with the process.

Susyn offers the kind of love that only a Godmother can offer, the kind that says, "I know it hurts, my love, I am here to be with you in pain, and when you are ready, I am here to guide you from the brokenness to healing."

The book you hold comes at the perfect time—not only for you, not only for your healing, but for the healing of the world. Our hearts are collectively breaking for the tremendous suffering of the billions of humans who live with life-shattering pain. Today, by walking the journey to healing your heart, you join a global community of fierce leaders who will, indeed, transform the world.

RYAN WEISS

www.WakingUpWithRyan.com

A WORD ABOUT WORDS

For me, the words God, Goddess, Source, Higher Power, Greater Field of Life, and Creator are all an expression of the all-inclusive Loving Energy of the Universe that flows through every being. It is this energy that is our co-creative partner in creating our greatest masterpiece—our lives. There are times that I write God as G-d; this is what I learned in Hebrew school about sixty years ago, and it captures the great mystery of God for me. If the words I use to express this universal energetic mystery, that connects beings don't work for you, please substitute your own. One of my coaching clients recently told me that the letters LO express her understanding of God, the Loving One.

In addition, there are times when I spell Love with a capital L. This is the Love that represents more than romantic love or loving a particular food, movie, activity. This is the Love that expresses our wholeness, our alignment in body-mind-spirit, and our birthright as mighty expressions of Love in the world.

HOW TO USE THIS BOOK

I wrote this book to guide you in freeing your heart and mind from brokenheartedness—whether you are experiencing the pain of a recent heartbreak or wounds of the past that continually disrupt and block the flow of Love in your life.

This isn't a book to simply read and put back on your bookshelf. Rather, I am making a bold assumption that if you are now reading these pages, you are ready to digest the information and take action by completing the practices described throughout the book.

Ultimately, this is a feel-good book, but to experience this Loving place within, you have to allow the painful beliefs and feelings that generate your brokenheartedness to surface to the light of conscious awareness so that they can be transformed and healed.

I suggest you take your time to use this book rather than simply reading to get through it. To experience the greatest value, combine the concepts with action. As we all know, walking the talk requires action.

Some of the concepts presented may challenge the way you view the world. I encourage you to be curious—open your heart and mind to all points of view, regardless of whether or not you initially agree with them. Allow yourself to be mindful of the emotions, memories, and thoughts that surface when reading the book and doing the exercises.

REMEMBER: Resistance to any of the concepts or practices is usually a good indicator that you have opened a wound or scar. Generally, the more strongly you disagree with a particular idea, the greater your attachment is to your particular point of view—and the greater your gift when you let it go. And always remember, your intuition, your inner wisdom, is *your* best guide for your heart healing.

You will notice that some of the concepts are repeated multiple times. This is because the concepts build upon one another, and repeating them helps to clarify their meaning, deepen your understanding, and expand your point of view.

Whenever you are ready to open the book, first identify your particular intention. Consider the following suggestions or use your own:

- I choose to know what is most important for me to learn about heart healing and forgiveness now.
- How do I open my heart and trust Love?
- How may I courageously expand my capacity to forgive?
- Show me how to reframe these circumstances from a new Loving perspective.
- Give me the courage to free my heart and mind from the pain of heartbreak.
- What would Love do here?

The book contains three main sections:

I. My Personal Heart Healing Story

II. The Concepts: Heart Healing and the Power of Forgiveness

III. Practicing Forgiveness

Here are three specific suggestions for using this book—choose one or use the combination that works best for you:

1. **Start at the beginning,** focusing on one chapter at a time. If there are exercises in the chapter, complete them. Use a personal journal to write your reflections, questions, challenges, insights, and the "aha" moments you experience while reading the chapter.

2. **Open the book at random,** reading the page you opened to. If there is an exercise, do it. If there are multiple exercises, choose the one that is most relevant to you.

3. **Create a Heart Healing Circle** and use this book as its curriculum. Invite your family members, friends, or members of your church, mosque, synagogue, spiritual community, or book club to join you. (See Heart Healing Circle Format in the Appendix, page 185.)

INTRODUCTION

Dear Reader,

I love getting letters. I encourage you to read this letter as though it is a personal invitation to heal your heart of heartbreak and wounds of the past. Keep in mind that a healed heart is a whole heart—a heart that has weathered those broken places so the light of Love from within easily flows out, and the Love from outside easily flows in.

I have felt a great responsibility in writing this book. I am an elder. I have sixty-nine years of experience being a human, and I have had the blessing and privilege throughout my life of working with tens of thousands of people who have invited me to guide them through life challenges that had left them angry, hopeless, and filled with regret, shame, the desire for revenge, and resentment. Also, since the time I was a child, close family members and friends have sought my guidance when seduced by anger, wounds of the past, and a deep desire for greater Love, happiness, and peace of mind in their lives.

You can't connect the dots looking forward; you can only connect them looking backward. So you have to trust that the dots will somehow connect in your future.
—Steve Jobs

The question that fuels my life is one I wrote in my journal as a teen: *What would the world be like if everyone loved themselves?* In retrospect, I now know that this question, penned by the fourteen-year-old me, was an invitation to my life's work—my Calling—and the point of view that our relationship with ourselves forms the blueprint for all the relationships in our lives.

These days, I express this Calling through the title of Godmother—this is my way of sharing the wisdom of experience and being a mighty expression of Love. Earlier in my life, there were other professional titles, including organizational development consultant, executive coach, interfaith minister, life coach, and self-esteem expert. Then there are the personal roles: child, daughter, sister, wife, stepmother, single woman, friend, lover, and grandmother.

Through the wealth of experiences that a long life offers, I have come to know that a healed heart—an open heart—is necessary to feast on the gifts of your one precious life, as well as for a more Loving, peaceful, accepting, compassionate, and caring world. There are moments when it seems so simple to me—we are all going to die anyway, so why not enjoy the journey during our brief time on Earth, and heal our hearts, free ourselves of the wounds of the past (personal, generational, and cultural), and commit to allowing Love to illuminate our time here?

Knowing the pain of heartbreak and the opportunity it always presents for healing, I wanted to write a book that would be immediately engaging and ultimately, in my biggest dream, would also be a catalyst for millions of readers to hone their dealing, healing, and forgiving skills and to say, "Yes" to being mighty expressions of Love in the world.

Even though I had a big dream for this book, it was challenging for me to write. I was very much in Love, and brokenheartedness seemed to have been in my distant past. After being single for 15 years, I was in a relationship that nourished me spiritually, emotionally, physically, and intellectually.

After a few months of dating and feeling at home with this very special man, he invited me to move in with him. My response was an immediate "Yes," as every cell of my being was jumping for joy.

We made our home on a beautiful lake, sharing morning walks, mouthwatering meals, and laughter as we imagined dreams we would share together. Being with Beau, I truly felt more open to giving and receiving Love than I had ever before in my life.

"Where do I begin?" I wondered when more often than not I simply wanted to be with Beau. But a deadline was looming, so in meditation, I repeatedly asked myself, 'What is heart healing?' Following the thread of responses I heard, I completed the manuscript as I continued to deepen and expand my capacity to be, give, and receive Love.

As I put the finishing touches on the manuscript, Beau was preparing for a trip to China, in part to explore places for us to live and visit during a year of traveling in Asia that was to begin in January 2018.

On the morning of May 4, 2017, I was excited to receive an email from Beau. I was not expecting my world to change as I clicked to open the email. Hello, heartbreak, I had hoped never to meet you in this relationship.

While my heart healing catalyst was the unexpected and abrupt ending of a loving relationship, there are many other life challenges that trigger heartbreak. This confronts us with the choice of closing our hearts or stepping fully onto the courageous path of not only healing our current heartache, but also freeing our hearts and minds of the wounds of the past.

Whether your heart healing journey has been triggered by the end of a relationship, the death of a loved one, a devastating health diagnosis, a financial crisis, addiction, career challenges, or the myriad other circumstances that generate feelings of victimization, anger, resentment, guilt, shame, fear, anxiety, and hopelessness, you can apply the practices of forgiveness that fill this book to open your heart to Love.

It is our heartbreaks that are a direct call for heart healing. And if there is anything that our world is calling for right now, it is Love—in our personal lives, our families, our workplaces, our communities, and the larger world we share with all beings.

Now, if you are ready to heal your heart and open your life to Love, take a full, cleansing, deep breath and say the Prayer for Wholehearted Living aloud as an expression of your commitment to healing your heart and being a mighty expression of love in the world.

With all my Love,

Susyn

Prayer for Wholehearted Living

From *The Wholehearted Life*

Today I live a wholehearted life. I easily let go of my attachment to thoughts and behaviors that block the inflow and outflow of Love in my life. I know my purpose is to be a mighty expression of Love in the world through expressing and generously offering my unique gifts, talents, and skills for the highest good of ALL. I trust that every experience I have is an opportunity to deepen and expand my capacity to be, give, and receive Love. I ask for and receive all help available to me, visible and invisible, to easily and effortlessly learn from and release habit patterns of fear, blame, and separation, have faith in a Loving future, and live fully and wholeheartedly in the Precious Present.

For the eternal peace and happiness for all.

And, it is so…

PART I:

MY PERSONAL HEART HEALING STORY

May 2017–May 2018

INTRODUCTION

What is most personal is most universal.
—Carl R. Rogers

I'm sharing my heart healing story at the beginning of this book, not because it is unique, rather because I know the power of stories. As you read mine, I imagine you will be reminded of similar feelings you have had or are having in the midst of a broken heart. You will see that while our circumstances are different, we share some or all of the emotions and thoughts activated by heartbreak—and in this, I pray that you will know that you are not alone.

You will also see that healing a broken heart is not a linear process. For instance, if your heart initially closes as a way of protecting you from the devastating onrush of pain, and then over time opens, this doesn't mean that your heart may never close again. It is through waking up to our beliefs—thoughts charged with emotional energy, thoughts that have been thought over and over again—that we learn what triggers our physical sensations and emotions and that we uncover the programming (the operating system) that informs our life. It is through this awareness that we can choose to accept the invitation to upgrade the software of our mind and heal our heart.

I have had the gift of working with and guiding thousands of women and men as they navigated the pain of heartbreak to heal their hearts and find the courage to boldly Love again with audacity. I share my journey with you so you will know that Love is your birthright and see that ultimately a broken heart is an open heart—allowing the light of Love to flow in and out.

You didn't just break my heart; you broke our future.
—Steve Maraboli

On May 2, 2017, I eagerly awaited the return of Beau, the man I loved. He'd been in China for three weeks. We had dreamt about Asia and were planning to live and travel there beginning in January 2018 for at least a year. China and tea had captured his heart.

I was delightfully imagining the sexy lingerie I'd wear to greet him upon his return and the food I would have ready for him. I knew what made his mouth water.

♥ May 3, 2017 ♥

I hadn't heard from Beau during the previous two days. When we had last spoken on Sunday, he'd said he'd be up in the mountains for a few days and didn't expect to have Wi-Fi or cell service.

I had called Beau as soon as I had gotten home on Sunday after leading a two-day workshop in New York City, where I had listened intently to thirty interfaith seminary students, then taken a four-hour trip back to Massachusetts.

He was distressed as he told me that while the people he loved lived in the United States—his three kids, four grandkids, and ME—the country he loved and that was calling to him was China—7,000 miles away. After about fifteen minutes of listening, I lovingly said, "Beau, I know this is important to you, and I want to listen, but I've been listening to thirty people for two full days—I have to go to sleep." I'd sensed annoyance in his voice as he said, "Okay, go to sleep."

I hung up the phone, but a few minutes later, I called him back. I so wanted to be there for him. Isn't this what we do for those we Love? He spoke more about his internal struggle. After about twenty minutes, I was shocked to hear myself blurt out, "Are you breaking up with me?" Without missing a beat, he said, "No, our relationship is good." But during the two days since, while I hadn't heard from him, I had wondered why I had asked that question out of the blue. I'd wished I could take it back. While I didn't obsess about it, sporadically throughout the day, it had popped into my mind. Then I remembered, he had reassured me that our relationship was good.

♥ May 4, 2017 ♥

I woke up very excited that Beau would soon be home. It was a beautiful sunny May day. Watching the sunlight dancing on the pond from the bed that Beau had bought just for us, I envisioned our bodies entangled like spaghetti—delighting in the view we were so blessed to wake to each morning. A delicious morning of lovemaking had taken hold of my imagination. He would be home in just five days.

An hour later, as the morning sun filled the living room with the glorious light of a new day, I was sitting on the couch with my laptop on my lap, not expecting my world to change when I opened my email. This is what I read:

I am back on my path. The path I was on when we met. Our love filled my life with joy. I thought it was my new path to be with you...but over here I have seen my way again. And I have realized it is my way, not our way.

There is not much else to say except I have been blessed by your presence for the time you were with me.

But now I must set out again on the road that I was on.

I wish you all the best—bestselling books, novels, special friends, full happiness, bliss.

I will be back on May 9. I have things to wrap up and to prepare for an extended time in Asia. I do not think it will be a good time for us to be sharing my house as I will be in the process of wrapping up my time on the pond. Getting ready for my water to be the Mekong, the Yangtze, the South China Sea, Lake Lugu...

All my love and best wishes,

Beau

In the thirty-five seconds it took for me to read the email, my life changed. I stood up, clutching my laptop. As I looked around the room, nothing seemed real to me. There it was, that feeling I hated—being cast out. Pain coursed through me as though I had been stabbed with a rusted jagged edged dagger, right in the center of my heart. My chest collapsed, and my breath got caught in my throat. Hello, heartbreak, I had hoped never to meet you again.

In the midst of this shock, unable to move, II heard these words, loud enough to hear and clear enough to understand, directly from my now broken open heart, 'Obviously, this is the best he could do;' and 'What is it about me that has me once again experiencing this feeling of being cast out?'

I moved through the day in a fog. It was as though I had been surgically exorcised from my life, a life that was safe, familiar, and filled with love, visions, and dreams that made my heart sing. Even though my physical environment hadn't changed, I no longer had a place in it.

I was now in the midst of my very own heartbreak, and the irony did not escape me. I had just, three weeks earlier, completed my new book about heart healing. Now I had some big dealing and healing to do.

I was furious each time I reread Beau's email. Best wishes!! Are you out of your fucking mind, Beau! Today was up there with the worst days of my life. Everything that had felt safe and known to me was no longer a solid foundation I could depend on. One thing I knew for sure was that I didn't plan to be moved out of here in five days. I was the one who had turned this place, where Beau had lived in monk-like fashion, into a home.

Somehow, I managed to put one foot in front of the other—thank goodness for the power of shock.

I didn't want to call and tell anyone, because then this horrible nightmare would be real. Everything in me wanted to go back to an hour ago when I saw that Beau had sent me an email. I was so excited to open it and read about his time in the mountains of China and his new tea discoveries.

After sitting so still that all that seemed to be moving was my breath and the blinking of my eyes, I called Josie. We'd been friends for eight years and had spent endless hours in her hot tub talking about men. She had truly been the wind beneath my wings when I knew it was time to end my previous relationship. We hadn't spent a lot of time together since Beau had captured my heart, although we'd spoken a few times a week while she was in Florida for the winter. She regularly commented about how special it was to be with us. Love was contagious around us. She loved seeing me joyously and happily in love. As soon as she said, "Hi," I started bawling.

"What's wrong? Suze, what's happened?"

"Beau broke up with me in an email an hour ago."

"That fucker. What's wrong with him? Come down here, stay with me. We'll drive from Florida back to the Berkshires together."

As I continued to weep, I managed to say, "I'm going to call Calla and ask if I can stay the weekend at her house." Through a barrage of tears, barely able to catch my breath, I mumbled, "I have to get off the phone. I'm miserable."

"Susyn, you know you can call me anytime, day or night. I can't believe this is happening to you. What the fuck is wrong with him? In an email! I love you. There are so many people who love you."

"Bye, Josie," I said.

As though moving through quicksand, I got dressed and made my way to my appointment with my osteopath for the pain in my hip that had begun a few weeks earlier. Once in the examining room, she asked, "How are you today?" I immediately dissolved into tears, and while gulping for breath, told her, "I got an email this morning from my boyfriend breaking up with me and telling me to move out before he arrives home in five days. He has been in China for a few weeks."

As she expertly manipulated my body to relieve my physical discomfort, she encouraged me to allow my emotions to flow. I did. Thirty minutes later, when I got up from the table feeling some physical relief, she hugged me as her words momentarily soothed my distress, "You've had a terrible shock. What a cowardly way to end your relationship. Take care of yourself. You don't have to make any decisions right now." Taking a deep breath, I left the examination room, feeling grateful for my now pain-free hip.

I drove home in a daze, knowing that I had to get away. I wished there was some way for me to step out of my life.

Back at the house, I called Calla. She was shocked as I read her Beau's email. She had visited us a few months earlier and had seen how happy and loving we were together. As my tears flowed and my heart ached, I asked, "Will you be home this weekend? Can I come to your house tomorrow and stay for the weekend?" Her response was immediate, "Of course you can. Come right now." Barely able to speak, I whispered, "I'll be there in the morning. Bye."

My new friend Mary was coming over for dinner. She didn't know what she was stepping into!

I started to prepare dinner by rote, first measuring the rice and getting the rice cooker going, then chopping the ginger, garlic, and scallions for the stir-fry. I'd cooked hundreds of nourishing, healthy, mouthwatering meals in this kitchen. During our first few months together, Beau was often surprised that I loved to cook. Tonight, cooking captured my attention. For a while, my tears stopped, until the moment Mary opened the door and walked into the house.

"What's wrong?" the words shot out of her mouth.

"Beau broke up with me in an email this morning."

Looking at me quizzically, she asked, "Did you have any idea this was coming?"

"No," I declared as a fleeting memory crossed my mind of the question that had jumped out of my mouth during our last conversation, "Are you breaking up with me?"

Sitting down to eat, I had no appetite. I moved the food around my bowl, the bowl Beau and I had bought together. Everything I saw and touched elicited a memory as my eyes welled over and over again with tears. Mary kept reminding me to take care of myself, to be gentle with myself, and to allow my feelings to flow. When we finished eating, she went home. I was drained and just wanted to get under the covers and hide.

I crawled into our bed, the bed he had bought for us because he loved me, he loved us.

When first faced with heartbreak that pulls the rug out from underneath us, and when the life we know is radically changed, putting one foot in front of the other is an accomplishment. Here are actions to consider and take to deal with the immediate shock:

- Acknowledge and allow your feelings to flow. (They may include rage, anger, numbness, disbelief, hurt, abandonment, hopelessness, fear, shock…)
- Be gentle with yourself.
- Reach out and share what you are experiencing with a trusted family member, friend, or professional, or express what you are feeling in a journal.
- Ask for what you need from trusted family and friends (for example, may I stay at your house; please don't give me advice unless I ask for it; hug me, allow me to feel my feelings…)

❤ May 6, 2017 ❤

At this moment, I am heartbroken. The irony is my new book is titled *Heart Healing*! I am empty. This morning, I hated Beau for the cruel email he sent to me ending our relationship. In brief moments of clarity, of course I know that if he could have done better, he would have. This was the best he could do. I wondered, why would I want to be with a man like this?

I'm an empty vessel. The good news is that I have no appetite, so the seven pounds I gained over the winter will easily be gone. Heartbreak is my unexpected weight loss plan!

I stepped into life with Beau wholeheartedly. I was reveling in the glorious feeling of having a home again; not the house we were in, but the feeling of home that I so greatly loved, cherished, and immediately felt with Beau. The rug has been pulled out from underneath me.

My first memory of this feeling of being cast out is when I was three years old; when my mom went to the hospital, I was sent to my grandparents. I was the only one sent away; my two older sisters stayed home with my dad. Yes, my grandparents loved me, but I had never been away from my family—or even away from home before, and leaving my mother as she cried in the huge New York City hospital was scary.

This is the only part of what I remember from my time at my grandparents. (My nighttime ritual with my mom was to go into the bathroom, and when I sat on the toilet, she would turn on the faucet to help me pee before bed.)

In the bathroom alone at my grandparents', I'd turned on the faucet before sitting down on the toilet at bedtime. Within moments, my grandmother came in, and I imagine that what she said in her Eastern European accent was something like, "No need to have the water running." As the flow of water stopped, I felt myself disappear. My familiar nighttime ritual was now gone—everything I was familiar with was gone. I was away from my home, my parents, and my sisters for the first time in my life. At that moment, I closed my heart in a treasure chest bound with chains and a padlock with the key nowhere to be found. I stopped eating and talking. My grandparents drove me home many days before my mom returned from the hospital.

♥ *May 7, 2017* ♥

It is interesting to me that, for decades, I remembered a poem I first read in a literary book written by students in my elementary school about a treasure locked away in a secret garden. My memory of the exact words of the poem dissolved as my heart opened on a spiritual journey with Don Miguel Ruiz in 2002.

On that day, I had been emotionally distraught and unable to free myself from the certainties that I was doomed to forever feel my *I'm not enough* and that I would never truly experience Love. The poem, which I had first read in elementary school and immediately learned by heart, had been playing through the echo chamber of my mind throughout that day.

As we sat in an amphitheater amidst the pyramids of Teotihuacan, Don Miguel, who was down below on the stage, asked, "Who is afraid of me?" I was drawn to him. In what I can only describe as a trance, I walked down the seats of the amphitheater and stood before him. I remember him gazing straight into my eyes.

After some time, he turned to our Dreamers group and said, "I'd need a lot of Viagra to get through to her." I had locked away my heart so deeply and for so long; I was embarrassed and ashamed by what he said about me. I continued to be transfixed as I held his gaze. Then I collapsed, I swooned as my eyes closed. I had swooned, and my eyes closed. When I opened my eyes again, my head was cradled in the lap and arms of Gary. He was whispering to me softly over and over again, "You are beautiful. You are Loved." It was as though I had been reborn. After a time, I was helped to stand up. My legs were wobbly.

I felt like a clean vessel. No more constriction, my heart had opened. The treasure chest was unlocked. Later that day when we were walking on the road to another site, I ran like the wind. My body—my very being—was spacious.

On our last day at the pyramids, we climbed the steps to the Pyramid of the Sun, where man becomes God. I realized as we sat at this portal that I was also one with the pilot who flew a plane into the World Trade Center on September 11, 2001. I committed at that moment to never hating again. But yesterday morning, I hated Beau. It was not a screaming and yelling hate, calling him names and wanting everyone I knew to know what a horrible person he was; rather I felt a deep wound that his cruel email elicited.

Sunday you loved me—Thursday you were through with me. I'm not disposable. I openheartedly stepped into our relationship. I trusted we were planning a life together. I do not know what is going on with you. Did you meet an Asian woman who won't ask you questions, who could be a translator for you in China? Are you gay?

I do realize that your email was the best you could do. But I don't deserve to be cast out in an email that essentially says, "Leave my house, I have a new dream, and you are not part of it." I refuse to close my heart because you have treated me so cruelly… I refuse to believe that it is not safe to Love. I refuse to believe that you are my last chance at Love. I refuse to believe that I will not share a home with a loving man again.

What happened to our plans to travel and live in Asia? Why is this dream dead to you? What is going on? Why have you banished me from your life? You don't want conflict. You don't want to see me cry, be upset, be angry with you? Isn't it funny that one of the first things I said shortly after we met was, "You're a grown-up? I like that you're a grown-up." *Wow*, I am clearly a lousy judge of character. You ended our relationship in an email! Writing that there is nothing more to say, telling me to get out of your house in five days. This is not the way a grown-up who claims he loves me treats me. I deserve better. I deserve to know why you have cut me out of your life—surgically removed me with no anesthesia. What is going on with you?

I do not know why you have banished me and torn me out of this dream. Who are you? Don't you know that you are safe to share who you are with me?

But this writing isn't about you. It is about me upgrading the software of my mind so I know I can continue to trust, trust a man, trust Love.

When you told me that you would change your China plans when my gynecologist noticed something irregular in my left breast, I felt so cared for and so loved. A few days later, I told you I felt so safe and embraced by your love. While I don't remember your exact response, I sensed you felt I was a burden. I am not a burden. I deserve to be loved, cared for, and cherished.

What do I have to heal in me so I don't have to repeat this pattern, this pain of being banished, of being cast out that I felt when:

- Mom went to the hospital when I was three years old and I was sent to my grandparents

- B told me he didn't know if he was coming to my dad's funeral because he was in love with someone who was moving away

- G told me four days after I had an abortion that we had no future (an abortion I'd had because I feared he would leave me if I wanted a child)

- D, who would tell me to go to my office when I was annoyed—why was I always the one told to leave?

- D, who called and told me he was filing for divorce and that he'd be gone for the weekend, so I should move out of the house that we had lived in together for eleven years.

Now, this is what you have done since your dream is no longer our dream. You have cast me out.

Maybe you feel a sense of relief after having written that "Dear John" email to me. It seems like this is your M.O. in dealing with relationships; no talking to your ex-wives. Do you even know what LOVE is?

♥ May 8, 2017— 8:48 a.m. ♥

Calla and Fred are a godsend. They hugged me, listened to me, and fed me, and when I crawled under the covers for hours at a time, they checked on me every so often to see if there was anything I needed or wanted. Their Love turned the faucet of tears on, the kind of tears that let me know that it is safe for me to keep my heart open. But now I am going back to the cottage, back to that place that had been my safe loving home.

Letter to friends:

I am empty and heartbroken today, an empty shell. Beau ended our relationship in an email he sent from China. I am embraced by Calla and Fred's Love. Their home has been my refuge this weekend.

I'm going back to the pond today; it's hard to call it home, and I don't have the energy to talk…other than to write and ask for your prayers to hold me in the light so that I may see my way clear to living a life of Love, kindness, compassion, and joy—filled with a feeling of home.

I Love You,

Susyn

P.S. I am so grateful for all the Love in my life.

My heart is racing. I did the Healing Your Tender Heart Meditation, took a bath, weighed myself—the winter pounds have melted off. I'm eager to see my weight on the scale at home. *Home:* what is it? I told you, Beau, so many times how I loved the feeling of home that filled me to overflowing being with you. I made the cottage a home…that's what I do, I make homes, and I create Loving spaces.

The night before I left for San Francisco, two days before you were leaving for China, you wanted to make love. But you had been so dismissive of me that evening. We had made plans to go out. When I mentioned it to you, you said, "Go by yourself if you want." We were going to be apart for many weeks, more time than ever before. I wanted to spend this last night with you, but that wasn't important to you until we got into bed. But I was hurt and turned away from you numerous times when you reached out for me. There was no loving lovemaking that night. I apologized in the morning. When I left for the airport, we held one another, expressed our love, and I gave you the care package filled with treats I had lovingly made for you to take along as you embarked on your China adventure.

I'm not sure what I will say to you when we see each other. I wonder what your reaction will be to me still being in your house, the home we made together. I've thought that I might give you these journal pages to read—who knows, I will, or I won't.

I don't even know what time you are coming home. It's like when D and the kids were in Florida, when we were separated and still lived in the same house. Their flight had been delayed, and no one let me know. D said Kathy, the secretary who became his girlfriend moments before he told me to move out, was supposed to let me know. She didn't. She was jealous of me.

Last week you changed your flight plans, no discussion there. Who navigates a loving relationship this way? I was going to mention it to you, but not until you got home and we could talk. I imagined cuddly pillow talk when we would connect and feel safe to be vulnerable and share whatever was on our minds. This is the kind of conversation I am desperately hoping to have when you return home.

I'm leaving Calla's in a little while. It's probably a good idea for me to make one of my Done Lists—starting out by imagining that I will get these things done!

- Did laundry
- Returned library books
- Ate—even though I have no appetite and I feel sick to my stomach
- Did Healing the Tender Heart Meditation again
- Kept my *heart* wide open

♥ May 9, 2017 ♥

I cried a lot this morning. I had long conversations with Josie, Mary G., and Eve. Beau is supposed to be home sometime today. He hasn't been in touch. I have not contacted him. Should I have? Maybe I should have called him last week after I got the email and pretended I never received it? It's too late for that now. I don't know what time he plans to be here. I have plans to be out this evening.

I'm leaving him a letter on the kitchen counter. I spoke to Rikk, I wanted a man's point of view. He helped me get clear about what I wanted to say. I am so grateful for his friendship. Conversations with him across 3,000 miles always feel like a Loving embrace. Here's the letter I'm leaving for Beau.

Dear Beau,

You may be surprised that I'm still here.

I'm here because I opened my heart to you unconditionally. I said, YES, and committed to sharing our lives together. Before moving in with you, I promised I wouldn't leave you, that I would care for you.

As you might imagine, I'm heartbroken, confused, and hurting. At the same time, I sincerely want to hear what led to the email you sent to me last week (though not tonight after your long day of travel). I believe the Love we share is strong enough to allow us to truly share words from our hearts—face to face.

I'll be back between 8:30 and 9:00 p.m.

Love,

Susyn

What I know for sure based on my personal experience of freeing my heart and mind from blocks to Love and of working with thousands of clients is:

- At every moment each of us is doing the very best we can based on the software of our mind that is often beneath our conscious awareness.
- A current heartbreak is amplified by any unresolved, unhealed wounds of the past.
- When in the throes of heartbreak, be open to memories of similar experiences from other times of your life.

> **REMEMBER:** A current heartbreak that feels similar to past experiences is not evidence that you are not enough and that Love, happiness, peace of mind, and gratitude are not in the cards for you. Rather, current heartache allows old wounds to come to the light of your conscious awareness; it allows you to wake up to the beliefs you have about yourself, romantic relationships, and Love; and it allows you to heal your heart to give and receive Love more deeply and fully than ever before. This is what it means to be healed—your heart is open to the inflow and outflow of Love.

♥ *May 17, 2017* ♥

So much has happened during the past nine days. Right now, I feel like an empty shell, as if I am going through the motions of life simply doing only what must be done. But I'm not completely empty because there are tears still pouring out of me throughout the day. I wonder if tears and an endless leaking of snot lead to weight loss. Maybe if I cry enough and blow my nose enough, I will disappear… At times, disappearing seems like a good option to me.

Yesterday, I had fleeting moments of clarity. First, I decided to focus all my attention on getting my heart healing book out into the world. I had a purpose. I thought that this break-up story had to be part of the book. Then I wondered if I even want this new book published. I spoke with the publisher, and we agreed to speak again in July to decide what to do.

In less than two weeks, everything I felt happy and secure about—my relationship with Beau, our home, summer plans on the pond, my excitement about getting my book *Heart Healing* published, living and traveling in Asia with Beau next year—has evaporated. Here I am, sixty-eight years old, in debt, and I don't know where to live. Why is this happening to me?

My new year's resolution this year was again to *surrender*. Surrender more deeply than ever before to trusting the Loving Energy of the Universe. My mantra G-d/Love is my Source-Supply-Support, and I Am blessed and grateful.

Beau didn't come home on Tuesday, May 9. I looked pretty that day. I felt calm. The next morning, there was an email from him:

> *I should have been more direct in my previous email.*
> *By saying "I do not want to share my house with you," I meant that I do not want you there when I return.*
> *I am returning this evening.*
> *Please allow me the space of my home.*
> *Thank you.*
> *Beau*

It was another dagger in my heart. Tears flowed and flowed, and my heart ached. I went to my Emerging Woman art class; tears and art. When I got back to the house (no longer my home, he had made that clear in his email of that morning), he was asleep. I sat down to do some work on my computer, but I was captivated by the birds at the feeder and already missing this pond that I had come to Love. I went to the library to get a novel to get lost in. When I returned to the house, he was in the kitchen in his bathrobe, making tea.

"Can we talk?" I managed to ask.

He said, "Yes."

"What happened?"

He began to tell me about his plan to return to China, his solo plan to teach English and be a tea merchant.

"What happened to us?" I blurted. "What happened that on Sunday you loved me and on Thursday I opened an email that read, my way is not our way?"

Barely looking at me, he continued, telling me that before we met, he'd planned to return to China alone. He had never followed his dreams, what was truly in his heart. Looking back on twenty-five years as a corporate executive, while there were some satisfying parts to it, it was not truly who he is.

"What about our conversations about being in Asia together? What about our conversations about you finding a place for us to live there next year?" I asked.

His reply was, "I don't remember that, I didn't think it would happen."

"But you texted me from China, telling me about places we might live. Why don't you want me to go?"

"I want to do this alone. It's too hard to be in a new culture where I don't know the language yet and have to make decisions with you: where to go, what to eat. We haven't even traveled together." He didn't know what a great traveler I am.

"But you were in China with someone else, with Jamie."

"But that's different. Our relationship wasn't working for me. I wasn't feeling happy. You should have known when I didn't want to go to San Francisco with you. Things were emotionally difficult for me. It wasn't that way for you. I should have told you."

Then my anger got the best of me. I was screaming and yelling, crying hysterically. I went into our bedroom and slammed the door. Curled up under the covers, I fell into a deep sleep. Upon awakening in the wee hours of the morning, I heard him in the kitchen. I opened the door, walked toward him, and apologized for screaming.

"Do you want tea?" he asked.

"Yes."

Tea in hand, we went into the den and sat. We talked and cried. He held me; I sank into his embrace. We moved into the living room, and he made more tea for us. I had more questions for him.

"Did you meet someone you want to be with over there? Are you gay?"

"No. This is something I have to do alone. We cannot be boyfriend and girlfriend anymore. If we are, I won't be able to leave you, and I have to do this."

As I sat on the sofa listening to him, everything in me wanted to go over to the chair he was sitting on and hold him as his tears made their way down his cheeks. But he had just made it clear that he didn't want a physical relationship with me anymore. So I remained where I was sitting. I wonder if things would have turned out differently if I had gone to him and held him.

Emotionally drained, I went into the bedroom. A few minutes later, I opened the door, as he continued to sip his tea. I asked, "Would you come in and hold me?"

He did, and as I relaxed into the comfort of his familiar embrace, I hoped he would stay, and all would be right with us, we would again be *us*. About twenty minutes later, he left our bed without a word and went into the guest room.

I woke alone in our bed. Sunlight sparkled on the pond. My heart ached. My misery was all consuming. I called Calla and asked if I could come for the weekend again. Knowing that I had a plan for the next few days, I walked out of the bedroom and saw Beau in the kitchen; it was tea time once again.

As I looked at him with my heart wide open, I said, "I'm going to Calla's for the weekend." Taking a deep breath as tears began to spill out of my eyes, I looked straight at Beau and said, "Last night as I listened to you tell me amid tears that you have to return to Asia alone, that this is your dream, that our relationship is too hard for you, that the painful emotions it has brought to the surface are old ones that you don't want to deal with, that if you allow yourself to be my boyfriend, you won't be able to leave me—every bit of me wanted to hug you and hold you so you would know that you are loved, that it is safe to be you with me. But you told me that you didn't want to have a physical or sexual relationship with me. I wanted to respect what you had said, so I held back. But I have made a commitment to myself—I will not allow this to close my heart. I will not give up on Love. I will not stop myself from expressing Love."

I packed and left once again by myself and headed to the home and hugs of friends who Loved me unconditionally.

On the drive to Calla's, I made some calls. It was time to let those closest to me know about this unexpected and devastating turn of events in my life. Each call was met with shock and a new onrush of tears streaming down my face. Lynn offered her lake house, which was about five miles from where I had lived with Beau. Relief—I had an immediate plan for a beautiful roof over my head. Josie was on her way up from Florida. Her tenants wouldn't be out of her home (Chestnut Lodge) for another two weeks, so she'd be living with me 'til then. Yes, Love/G-d is my Source-Supply-Support. I have a beautiful place to live, and a dear friend will be with me.

I woke at Calla's the next day unable to walk. The pain in my hip was worse than it had ever been. I spent two days in bed, making it to the bathroom when necessary by practically crawling.

On Sunday night, I drove to meet Josie at my new "temporary home."

Monday morning, while I was unsure of when I'd see Beau again or move my things out of the house, Katherine Woodward Thomas, the author of the New York Times best-seller *Conscious Uncoupling: 5 Steps to Living Happily Ever After*, popped into my mind. Since I didn't have a copy of her book with me, I decided to make up my own steps to uncoupling. Here they are, "The 4 Keys to Open the Door to Heart Healing After Heartbreak":

•

KEY 1: TRANSFORM YOUR EMOTIONS

Acknowledge and allow the potent emotions you are feeling (including rage, fear, hatred, and desperation) to transform their destructive power from hurt and harm to being stepping stones to a lasting positive shift.

After reading Beau's break-up email, my anger flared, so much so that I wanted to take a pair of scissors and cut the bespoke blue blazer he loved into shreds. After decades of spiritual practice, even in the midst of escalating rage, the still small voice within spoke loud enough for me to hear and clear enough for me to understand, "Breathe, Susyn, I *AM* with you." Rather than getting the scissors, I walked out to the pond, and through a series of bellowing screams, released my anger. I assure you that there was more anger, rage, and despair in the days and months ahead; but at that moment, after my screams and tears, though I felt drained, I knew that the wisdom of my heart always offers the most Loving wisdom. By acknowledging and allowing myself to really feel my emotions, rather than being seduced by the story surrounding the break-up email, my tears and screams were an outlet for the intense energy that was pulsing through my body. For a time, I truly felt at peace in the present moment.

•

KEY 2: KEEP YOUR ATTENTION ON YOURSELF

Rather than being seduced and entangled in a labyrinth of thoughts focused on your ex-partner and his/her cruel and reprehensible words and actions, focus your attention on yourself. What role did you play in the break-up? Do not approach this question from the point of view of blaming yourself.

Rather, what are your beliefs about relationships and Love? Do you believe to be loved that you must over-give, forego your dreams and needs, or sabotage yourself into believing that you are not worthy or deserving of true love? Your willingness to explore these questions opens the door to healing your current pain and suffering, as well as wounds of the past.

When you let go of being victimized by the words and actions of your ex-partner and commit to forgiving and releasing formerly unconscious habits of thought and behavior, you naturally reclaim your power as you deepen and expand a Loving relationship with yourself.

To be honest, I resisted this idea, even though I had written the step! I kept thinking, "But this came out of the blue. I didn't expect it. He told me repeatedly during our calls when he was in China how much he loved me." Then I remembered a thought that had popped into my mind after I had completed the *Heart Healing* manuscript, the one that might or might not ever be published!

I had been in the kitchen making tea, about ten days before his trip. He was angry with me that morning for some judgment he believed I was making about him. Quite honestly, the thought was simply in his mind, rather than being a thought I'd ever had. As I watched him walk out of our bedroom toward the bathroom, I heard these words as clearly as though someone was speaking directly to me, 'Maybe we have only been together for me to complete this book.' I'm not saying that this thought caused him to send me his devastating email, rather I had to admit that I had wondered if this was going to be my forever relationship. Did I want to be with a man who repeatedly assumed I was judging him when I wasn't?

•

KEY 3: OPEN YOUR HEART, HEAL THE WOUNDS OF THE PAST

Open your heart and mind to the origin of the wound story that has been recreated over and over again in your love life. "Repetitive compulsion" is the name Sigmund Freud used to describe our habit of repeating our deepest childhood traumas and hurts. Rather than using your current heartbreak as evidence that you will always lose in love relationships, shining the loving light of your conscious awareness on your wound story allows you to let it go and rewrite a new love story.

Within moments of reading Beau's email, I had thought, 'What is it about me that has me once again experiencing this feeling of being cast out?' I knew my origin wound story. It had taken root when I was three years old and sent to stay with my grandparents while my mom was in the hospital for surgery—my "cast out of the Garden of Eden" story.

While evidence I had gathered—over many decades of being cast out, through divorces, break-ups, and often feeling like an outsider—no longer elicited emotional pain and suffering, obviously remnants of the beliefs that triggered this cast out feeling were calling to be healed. It is the power of our beliefs that over and over again fuel our repetitive compulsion. Until we truly forgive both ourselves and others and experience the gift and lesson each heartbreak offers, the pattern repeats. I knew I was ready to be free of this old story of never truly being loved.

•

KEY 4: TRUST THE POWER OF LOVE

Know that you always have access to the power of Love. When we are connected to the energy of Love, we open ourselves to infinite possibility in the present moment. We are mindful of our choices, and rather than unconsciously and compulsively repeating patterns of the past, when we are in the presence of heartbreak, we allow the majestic power of Love to be our guide. We allow our hearts to direct and in-form our thoughts, words, and actions from the inside out. This is the power of Love to heal our hearts.

Simply recognizing that I always have access to the Loving Energy of the Universe filled me with hope. Not only did I know that I would heal from this difficult heartbreak, but I trusted deep in my heart that there would be even greater Love for me in the future.

I knew my healing had begun. While I wished Beau would play the roles of Lover, Friend, and my Forever Man, I knew that each choice I made had to be an expression of me Loving me, all of me—on the days heartache felt like a deep rabbit hole that I didn't know my way out of, as well as when my faith that Love is my Source-Supply-Support soared. I kept reminding myself that my relationship with myself forms the blueprint for all the relationships in my life. I vowed to Love all of me unconditionally.

❤ *May 22, 2017* ❤

Got back from a quick trip to the Hamptons to meet with realtors to sell my house. Josie and I left Stockbridge while it was still dark in the wee hours of Sunday morning, in time to get to the 10:00 a.m. Sunday service at the New Thought Spiritual Center of Eastern Long Island (NTSC). I always feel bathed in Love at NTSC. Nick & Joseph opened their guest house to us. Tears, tears, and more tears fell in the presence of all the Love showered on me.

I've learned something about tears. Tears are an expression of an open heart. It is when powerful emotions flow through us—whether loving emotions or raw heart-wrenching emotions—that our tears flow. So often people apologize for their tears, judging their tears as something to be hidden. I used to try to gulp back my tears—I wanted to be strong. I no longer apologize for mine. It's the other way around; the courage and the vulnerability to express our tears is an expression of strength.

There is a sacredness in tears. They are not the mark of weakness, but of power. They speak more eloquently than ten thousand tongues. They are the messengers of overwhelming grief, of deep contrition, and of unspeakable love.
—Washington Irving

As long as I continue to allow my feelings to flow, I know I will not carry the wound of this breakup with me as a scar…an issue I am confronted with over and over again.

I asked in meditation, 'How long will it take for me to heal from this heartbreak?' The answer was clear, 'Thirteen months.' Then I asked, 'Can I heal the wounds of the past that had me believing that I would never be loved?' The answer was again immediate, 'That's what you're doing right now.'

Thank you, Loving Energy of the Universe for being my Source-Supply-Support.

Good night.

♥ May 23, 2018 ♥

I made a big decision today. I chose the realtor to sell my house. I got myself into a real financial bind during the past few years. I owed more than I had. I'm looking into doing some part-time counseling to generate some regular cash flow.

I now know that the next chapter for my work—my work of art—is to be a champion for heart healing. I keep remembering the words I wrote in my journal 54 years ago, 'What would the world be like if everyone loved themselves?' I'm now ready to step out in the world and be a Love Warrior. I've been uncomfortable with the word "warrior" because it has the word war in it. Then I remembered the Warrior pose in yoga, and its meaning of being a spiritual warrior battling the universal enemy, self-ignorance—forgetting that we Are one, and that it is our personal demons of 'I'm not enough-ness' that are the ultimate source of suffering, heartache, and acts of violence.

The thought of marketing *Heart Healing* feels like a burden. My new idea is to ask friends if they'll invite people they know to their living room for me to give a workshop. I think I'll call it "Opening the Door to Heart Healing." And when I'm asked about my title, I'll courageously say, "Godmother, sharing the wisdom of my experience and being a mighty expression of Love in the world."

I feel a bit hesitant. Can I be a voice for Love when the man I Love rejected me? Whoa, I sure got a heavy dose of the programming that I don't count unless a man loves me… This is an old story, cancel, cancel—I know about Love. Yes, I do!

I'm feeling hopeful about life today.

Even in the midst of heartbreak, there are things we can focus on that bring us more firmly into the present moment and give us hope. What makes your heart sing? This doesn't mean that the pain of heartache is gone forever, rather that our heart song is a song of hope.

♥ June 3, 2017 ♥

Dear God,

It's been many months since I've written to you. Since you are my Source-Supply-Support, here are some of the things I'm committing to, and I need your help, because some mornings I just want to stay hidden under the covers:

- Go to the Nuns to meditate while they chant at 7 a.m. at least three times a week
- Write a Dear God Letter every day
- Eat healthy
- Great sex with a boyfriend I see two or three times a week
- Include my heart healing story in the *Heart Healing* manuscript

Letter to Beau (I probably won't send it, but it's helpful for me to write):

Dear Beau,

I Love you. This morning I read my Dear God letters from January and February—I was struggling with writing Heart Healing. *You assumed that I was making judgments about you and then took your assumptions personally—you were believing your assumptions; and it was also a loving, cozy, yummy food, laughter, spooning, Love making time.*

I wish you would be my boyfriend—we'd see one another once or twice a week until you leave in September. We'd share what's going on in our lives. We'd talk once a week while you're in China. I'd come to China in March to visit.

I turn this all over to you, God.

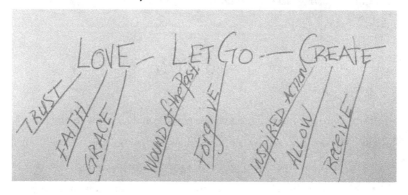

♥ June 4, 2017 ♥

Dear God,

I vacillate between no contact with Beau at all—from taking him off my daily Elevate inspiration mailing list (but I do like when I see he's opened my message) to feeling my ego soar when he responds with one word—"Sure"—when I ask if I can come over and we can have dinner together, or work on my computer.

I have a twinge of fear of growing old—alone in a small dark apartment, TV my main companion.

NO, NO, NO

God, guide me, I'm listening…

- *Focus on your body*
- *Stay in shape*
- *Go to the chanting nuns*

- *Schedule Heart Healing groups in friends' homes*
- *Follow up on counseling work*
- *Let him initiate*

Beau was not nice to me—he doesn't want to have sex with me (and who am I kidding, I only talked with him about friends with benefits because I want him to be my boyfriend). He doesn't want to see me—he said he'd make plans for us to go to the theater together, but he didn't do it.

I've got to stop being his cheerleader. But I am excited for him to live his dream.

I've got to stop wanting to give to him. He has made it quite clear that he doesn't want to work on his "stuff" in this lifetime. We couldn't even play backgammon together because he got upset when I frequently won.

I am <u>not happy</u>—I feel empty.

Help me, God, help me.

> *I am with you, Susyn, even now when you feel abandoned. I hear your wishes. I see the heart healing you are doing. Your wishes are being answered... Your friend, lover, companion is seeking you—he is on his way. Trust me, Susyn.*
>
> *Look at all the ways I am here for you: you have money, a great house to live in, health, and excitement about* Heart Healing. *Get your website done.*

💜 *June 5, 2017* 💜

Dear God,

Help me—I so very much, with every cell of my being, want to be in a committed, Loving relationship with a loving man. A man who is open to Love. One who can meet me in the depths and expansiveness of my Love.

As I'm writing, I am once again living the hangover of the emotional cocktail of equal parts very, very angry and heart wrenching pain. It's time to move my things out of Beau's, the cottage we shared together, a place where I was sooooo happy and a home where I felt so very loved.

But I hesitate to send him the text about packing my things up. I was hoping we would go out together to celebrate our anniversary of the day we met.

I have to let him go.

Oh God, help me work on the website and talk with the real estate broker to send me the papers to sign to get my house on the market.

Susyn—Know that all your prayers are being answered. To the degree you Love you—I assure you—a loving man is on his way to you. Now get on with your "work of art" to get Heart Healing *out into the world. Now is your time.*

♥ June 6, 2017 ♥

Dear God,

Susyn—See what happens when you acknowledge your feelings. You are more spacious, and more open to Love in the present moment. Larry, the realtor, responded, and the contract is signed. Beau asked you out for Friday night.

Keep Letting Go—Feel Your Feelings—Let Them Go
All of Them

- *Decide the dates for your Heart Healing groups.*
- *Talk to the friends who've offered their homes and write the invitations.*
- *Keep putting one foot in front of the other just as you have been doing.*

- *Regarding Beau, and your date on Friday. Be loving and true to yourself.*
- *Decide if you want him in your life.*

Why do I want Beau in my life?

- Known

- Yummy sex

- I felt I could count on him

- Do I even want him as a friend?

♥ June 7, 2017 ♥

The part-time counseling work is not going to happen. I don't have the certification needed, and the hoops to first find out about and then jump through them will take months, and I don't even know how long I want to stay in the Berkshires.

The good news is I fit into a size eight—it's been years. I feel so very comfortable in my body. I feel pretty and sexy.

There are times I've been wondering if Beau wants to be with me on Friday night, or if he just wants someone to go with him to this event. What am I believing when I question this?

- He's just using me

- He's not interested in me

- I'm just filler

- Men aren't interested in me

- I'm used by men

Susyn, you are a beautiful woman. You are interesting, fun, sexy, and desirable. Your Love is potent. People—men—want to be with you. Beau does love you. Is <u>he</u> enough for <u>you</u>? Be magnetic. Be authentic. Be you. When you question if *he wants to be with you and feel the empty feeling you are feeling now, connect with your younger self—your inner child. There she is right now, on a swing at the door of your open heart. See how your feelings change immediately when you acknowledge and feel your emotions. She is captivating. She is you. You are captivating. All you have to do is <u>be</u> <u>you</u>.*

💜 June 8, 2017 💜

After being at Beau's—the home we shared—where so much of my stuff and things still are, I left feeling empty. While I feel your presence, God, and I know that you are my Source-Supply-Support, there is a comfort for me in being at home with a man.

Yes, I must admit I did have questions in recent times if Beau was the man for me. I was aware of him being so annoyed with me about seemingly nothing; he regularly made assumptions that I was judging, criticizing, and having negative thoughts about him and then would get angry with me. He asked me many times to promise I wouldn't leave him.

I do like having a boyfriend. Or is it just the idea of having a boyfriend that I like?

Beau was here for me. I did feel loved, and for the first time ever, my capacity to receive Love was deeper and more expansive that ever before. I could count on him.

I just remembered that B told my dad that he would always take care of me. Well, that wasn't true. Here come the tears. Can I count on a man who tells me he loves me? Yes, I know I have to count on me—I have to Love me. I just remembered a time, years ago, when D and I were in the Landmark program, I stood up and said that I didn't know if I liked men. Not liking them and wanting a special one sure is a slippery slope.

Dear, dear God—I pray for all men's hearts to heal—and yes, of course, for women's hearts to heal, too.

Is tomorrow a date? Yes, I have a date with Beau tomorrow. I choose Love—Beau or better.

When old wounds surface, what beliefs have kept the pain of those wounds alive? This is where the healing takes place—through being mindful of our self-sabotaging thoughts, allowing the feelings they generate to be released, and to choose new thoughts that generate emotions aligned with our hearts' desire.

♥ *June 9, 2017* ♥

Dear God,

What advice do you have for me today?

- *Be you*

- *Listen*

- *Notice what you are feeling when you are with Beau*

- *Check in with me before he picks you up*

I am with you always. Turn to me when in doubt, when you are feeling empty, alone, sad, unsure, and angry. I am here for you. I AM Your Source-Supply-Support.

♥ *June 10, 2017* ♥

Dear God,

I'm feeling filled with peace.

Spent some time with Beau last night, not much to say.

I just scheduled two Heart Healing workshops. *Yay*, I'm doing it.

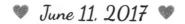 June 11, 2017

Dear God,

I'm at Calla and Fred's lake house. I can still feel Beau is so much a part of me. Last night, I wished I'd get a text from him. I wanted to text him—but I didn't. He made it clear he can't be friends with benefits with me. It's time for me to pay attention to his actions… and let go, let go, let go.

I am amazed by the way I am navigating this break-up. I am aware that there are so many unknowns before me, and I trust, dear God, that you are with me, illuminating the path.

June 12, 2017

Dear God,

Last night, I began imagining possible choices re: Beau—in no particular order.

- Let go of him completely. No contact. Get my things out of the house. Take him off the Elevate daily messages mailing list. Stop following him on Instagram.

- Keep seeing him as we are. Let him initiate our time together. Say goodbye in September. Do I go to Asia/China in March?

- Agree to see one another again in March.

I miss him. I wish he would be in touch with me. I am 68 years old, feeling the same way I did when a boy didn't call me when I was a teen. It sure is time to stop letting the absence of a call or text determine my feelings. Easier said than done! Better ask God.

Oh God, how do I let go of Beau as my boyfriend?

Stay connected with all of you—particularly the younger you, who for so long carried the wounds of believing she wasn't loved. See her right now; she is swinging on the swing through the open door of your heart. Allow yourself to feel the smile on your face. Regarding Beau—give him space. Trust that he did open his heart to you. He loved you to the degree that he can Love. Be true to yourself. Do you even want him to be your boyfriend? Focus on Heart Healing—*there is much to do and do soon. Direct your Love to this, now.*

♥ June 15, 2017 ♥

Dear God,

Yesterday was hard. I went to the house to pack up my things and the photos of us, along with the love cards and notes I had given him, were gone. I cried, and cried, and cried. I HATED him and again faced the question of 'do I let him go completely.'

I want to wake up from this nightmare.

Oh, I miss him so. I miss the *us* I imagine we could be if things were different than they are.

Susyn, this is your time to do your work—your work of art. Get Heart Healing out there. Trust that Love, romantic love, is on its way to you. Trust me, Susyn. I am with you. You are not abandoned.

♥ June 20, 2017 ♥

Dear God,

Please help me get out all the words I want to say. Help me express all the feelings this break-up has generated.

Dear Beau,

As I write this, I hate you. I hate that you sent me an email from China casting me out of your life with no conversation—*nothing*. **I am done with you**. Now that I am done with you—go off to China, be alone.

Why would I even want to celebrate the anniversary of our meeting? Maybe to put a bow around the package and close the chapter of Beau and Susyn.

There is *no* Susyn and Beau.

Yes, you did so many wonderful things for me—you were loving, caring, and generous, and I loved your gifts of flowers every week—and helpful, until you were ready to cast me aside. And that's what you did. You cast me aside.

I *hate you*—do you hear that *I hate you*?

I'm finished with you. Let me know when you're away from the house so I can get all my things out. So I can be another woman who you erase from your life.

I've learned that I am loving and I deserve to be loved unconditionally—not to simply be the object of your self-sabotaging projections. I'm eager for you to be a distant memory.

Fuck you, Beau

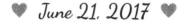 **June 21, 2017**

Dear God,

I just read the letter I wrote to Beau yesterday, and tears are falling on this page. There are other things I want to say...

I'm sorry that you:

- Didn't believe I *love* you
- Didn't feel safe with me

- Projected, projected, projected your lack of Loving yourself on me
- Ended our relationship in an email from China

God, how can I <u>not</u> make this choice again?

Susyn, you can trust me. Love is in the cards for you, and it is sooner than you think. You trusted his Love. Trust me; there is a loving man for you who also Loves himself. Continue to keep your heart open.

I'm glad I know not to mail these letters. They're such a good way to express my feelings and letting 'em go.

♥ June 22, 2017 ♥

Dear God,

I got an offer on my house today. I wanted to call Beau. I didn't. I'm glad I didn't, another step in letting go.

Thank you, God, for being my Source-Supply-Support.

A lot of changes in my life—more to come.

♥ July–September 2017 ♥

There were days I missed him as though a part of me was gone and all that was left was an empty space. I struggled with whether or not to take him off my Elevate daily inspiration mailing list—I did. Then I wondered if he even noticed. I moved all of my things out of his house. I led many "Opening the Door to Heart Healing" workshops and got a lot of great feedback, and I am thrilled with the design. I spent time with Beau many more times before he left in September to follow his dream. There were days I didn't think about him at all, and others when he seemed to have a long-term lease in my mind. The part of me that knows the importance of following the wisdom of our hearts truly celebrated his courage to follow his dream. There were many days that he inspired me with his clarity of focus to learn Mandarin, teach English, and discover fabulous Chinese teas. That's the kind of focus my *Heart Healing* work of art calls for.

Shortly before he left, I made him a gift that I asked him not to open until he arrived in China. It was a book of inspiring words and charms to remind him, on those days when he felt alone, that all is well. When I think about our goodbye the day he moved out of the house on the pond, I remember feeling his arms around me as we held one another in a robust bear hug embrace. Released from the hug (a moment of **h**eartfelt **u**nconditional **g**ratitude), gazing at one another, the last words I said to him were, "Remember, you Are Loved." He turned and walked back into the cottage.

When he got to China, he sent me photos and thanked me for the gift, and I received a group letter he emailed to family and friends. I think I was taken off the list… because there were no more to come.

He was on my mind a lot in the first few weeks after he left. The letting go continued. The question of whether or not I'd visit him in March popped into my mind with some regularity, but it was nothing I had to decide immediately. I had a house to empty.

❤ October 2017 ❤

I'm getting my Hampton Bays house ready for the closing on October 12th. I have at least fifty packed cartons that have been in the basement since I sold my East Hampton house in 2004. My tenants moved out on September 30th. Calla and Johanna will be here on October 4th, and when they leave on Friday, Robin will be here to help me get ready for the weekend moving sale. I have a lot of help from friends who Love me unconditionally—and are fabulous schleppers and great workers.

As I emptied the cartons, I didn't allow myself to get caught up in memory lane with each item until I got to the photo albums—from my childhood, teenage years, marriage to B, time with G, and marriage to D. As I looked at the photos, what became crystal clear is that I was pretty, I was thin, and I had boyfriends. The beliefs that had plagued me for decades that—I'm not pretty, I'm fat, I don't have boyfriends, I'll be the smart one—dissolved, as well as the "me too" experiences that further fueled those beliefs. The feelings of being unloved and cast out, that had taken root when I was three years old, were put to rest.

I began to realize that having felt so deeply loved by Beau and having my heart broken open so completely had given me the opportunity (you know, another one of those fuckin' consciousness expanding opportunities, it's like another level in a video game) to free myself—heal myself—of the old, old beliefs and wounds that had tormented me regarding Love.

♥ November 2017 ♥

I've decided to spend six weeks in San Miguel de Allende in mid-January to late February. I've rented a place, made my reservations, and contacted my friends who live there. There are moments I think of Beau and want to tell him what I'm doing. I don't. I no longer follow him on Instagram. I don't hear from him.

❤ November 22, 2017 ❤

San Francisco

As I began to do some holiday cooking, I was overcome with memories of Beau. I had to stop cooking; my tears were gushing. I sat down and wrote this letter… never to be mailed, yet I knew I had to allow the feelings to move through me.

> *Dear Beau,*
>
> *I'm in Maya's kitchen, ready to make cranberry sauce, and you showed up in my mind as though I was having a conversation with you.*
>
> *First and foremost, on Thanksgiving Eve, I'm grateful for the time we were a "we." Thank you for Loving me and being open to me Loving you.*
>
> *Last year at this time, we were in Love. I was sad for a bit that I wouldn't be with Maya, Kevin, Solange, and Rhone for Thanksgiving, but your Love embraced me, and our home felt like a warm hug. I made cranberry sauce then. That's such a loving memory for me.*
>
> *Anyway, I'm so curious about your life and imagine your heart is wide open to the dream you've created and continue to live into.*
>
> *I know your birthday is soon, so, Happy Birthday. May you celebrate and in-joy all your wishes—those you know and those yet to be revealed.*
>
> *Love,*
>
> *Susyn*

I got up, ready to get back to the cranberry sauce, then I quickly sat down again and wrote.

P.S. Sometimes, I <u>hate</u> you.

Then I felt ready to fill the cranberry sauce with Love.

I still have more heart healing to do, and I also have a great adventure before me. And best of all, my heart is wide open.

♥ December 2017—May 2018 ♥

My time in San Miguel de Allende was rich. I rediscovered that traveling alone opens a world of adventure, people, and many new experiences. Yes, there were moments I did wish I had a special man to share this with. Beau commented on some of my Instagram photos—so he was popping into my mind frequently, for a while. Every so often, I checked his Instagram page, but the time between the checking got longer and longer.

While in San Miguel Allende, I decided to do a memory lane road trip in the US during April and May to visit people who I hadn't seen in many years who have made a Loving contribution to my life. I moved out of the Stockbridge house and took to the open road—I had a plan, but this manuscript was still lingering.

♥ On Sunday, April 15, 2018 ♥

I am scheduled to deliver a sermon this morning at Unity Spiritual Center of San Francisco titled, "Wake Up to Sacred Dying." I woke quite early this morning—with Beau taking center stage in my mind-movie. After about 25 minutes filled with thoughts of him, I decided to check his Instagram. His father had died a few days earlier. I'd sent him a note thinking that I'd write more later about how I was speaking about death, and I thought of him, and he had recently posted about his dads' passing—ah, see how connected we are. Later in the day, I saw that he had written back to me, two simple words, "Thank you." There was no need for me to write more to him, we hadn't been in touch for months.

♥ May 4, 2018 ♥

It's now been a year since I received Beau's break-up email and I was faced with healing my broken heart. I remember the Loving note he'd left for me two weeks before I moved into the cottage on the pond. He had moved the desk I loved into the spot in the den with the best, *best* view of the pond. The note was waiting for me on the center of the desk:

Beau's Theory States
that this view will inspire you to the
best work of your life.
With all my love—Beau

My heart healing story is one of repeatedly waking up and of being aware and mindful of my programming so I could heal the wounds of the past; and one of ensuring that the ending of the Love story of Beau and Susyn would not become a wound of the past that blocked the flow of Love in my life, but rather a gift that opened my heart to Love more boldly than ever before.

COMPLETE THIS EXERCISE TO WAKE UP TO YOUR PROGRAMMING:

Fill in the blanks (You will most likely have multiple responses to what you are believing):

– When I am feeling [identify the emotion and the physical sensations], I am believing [about myself, others, life].

When you have recorded your beliefs, reflect on whether or not they are aligned with your heart's desire. If not, list the new belief—the upgraded program that supports your heart's desire.

PART II:

THE CONCEPTS: HEART HEALING & THE POWER OF FORGIVENESS

INTRODUCTION

I make a distinction between dealing and healing, both of which are integral aspects of healing our hearts through the undeniable power of forgiveness.

When your heart is initially broken, dealing is the task before you. This is generally the time when shock, numbness, and disbelief are in high gear. The world as you knew it no longer exists, even though your physical environment may remain the same. You may have responsibilities for children, family members, and work that do not allow you to hide and withdraw from your life. It is a time when you may wish to crawl under the covers and wake up back in your "old reality" before the heartbreak, or when you may be seduced by addictions. It is at this time that putting one foot in front of the other, brushing your teeth, eating, and getting dressed are huge accomplishments.

Dealing entails:

- Self-care

- Feeling your feelings

- Asking for and allowing the support, help, and Love of others

- Setting boundaries

REMEMBER: This is not a linear process with a specific time frame. Rather, it is a time when self-care is vital—and may very well feel like a burden.

While the tasks of dealing clearly contribute to healing, it is our commitment to healing that offers the opportunity to truly free our hearts and minds of the wounds of the past. When we only focus on the current heartbreak and do not open our awareness to the programming—the beliefs—we have about ourselves, others, life, and Love, we will continue to repeat painful, heartbreaking patterns.

Healing entails the same tasks as dealing, plus:

- Keeping your first attention on yourself—focusing on your thoughts, feelings, beliefs, and the patterns in your life.

- Practicing gratitude.

- Willingness to revisit, allow, and heal unresolved wounds.

- Curiosity about the gifts and lessons of the heartbreak(s) you have experienced.

- Committing to being impeccable with your words and always doing your best.

- Being of service to others, generously sharing your gifts, talents, and skills for the highest good.

●

CONCEPT 1: WHAT IS HEART HEALING?

A wound calls for us to recognize the hurt, to face the pain. Our honest expression gets the hurt out in the open, into the light, out of the darkness.
—Jennifer Williamson

As I began to meditate one morning, I posed the question, "What is heart healing?" The response was immediate, as though it was the voice of my heart, 'A healed heart is an open heart.' I opened my eyes to jot down this statement in my journal, and more questions, as though on automatic, quickly filled the page:

- What causes a heart to close?

- What's a broken heart?

- What's the difference between a closed heart and a broken heart?

- How do we open our hearts and minds to Love ourselves unconditionally?

- What causes a heart to open?

- Why is it so hard to live a wholehearted life of passion and purpose?

- How do we open and heal our hearts to experience Love more fully?

When the questions stopped, I began thinking about what happens to a physical heart when it is attacked. The United States Centers for Disease Control and Prevention reports that the most common type of heart disease is coronary artery disease, which constricts blood flow to the heart. Coronary artery disease is caused by plaque buildup in the walls of the arteries that supply blood to the heart and other parts of the body. Plaque is made up of deposits of cholesterol and other substances in the arteries. Over time, plaque buildup causes the inside of the arteries to narrow, which can partially or completely block blood flow. Decreased blood flow may then cause a life-threatening heart attack.

You may be wondering, 'What does this have to do with the emotional and spiritual pain and suffering I experience when I am heartbroken?'

The answer is quite simple. Most of us are walking around with wounded hearts from the pains, hurts, betrayals, regrets, shame, resentments, and anger attached to recent and past wounds. Each of these unhealed wounds—more importantly, the beliefs we have attached to them—constricts the flow of Love, of giving and the receiving, in our lives.

When the flow of Love is blocked, our hearts (emotionally, spiritually, and possibly physically) eventually become armored up or break. A broken heart generates feelings, which may include anger, fear, despair, rage, shame, and hopelessness.

Letting go of our attachment to the story of our wounds and to the beliefs that keep them oozing is the path to healing. It is an openhearted willingness to forgive ourselves and others, which is the emotional equivalent of the cardiac rehabilitation prescribed when someone experiences a physical heart attack.

•

CONCEPT 2: THE PROMISE OF HEART HEALING

For all darkness in the world stems from darkness in the heart. And it is there that we must do our work.
—Marianne Williamson

Heart Healing is an ever-evolving process of transformation—from a closed, wounded, armored, and conditionally Loving heart to an open heart in sacred union of mind-body-spirit aligned in conscious action. A healed heart is the evolution in consciousness—personal and collective—that calls to each of us to:

- Courageously allow ourselves to live an authentic life of passion and purpose.

- Acknowledge, celebrate, and contribute our unique gifts, talents, and skills for the greatest good for All.

- Know that the challenges we have faced and the hardships and pain we have experienced are gateways to greater Love, compassion, and kindness for ourselves and others.

A healed heart is rooted in the awareness that connection matters more than anything—connection with the G-d of our understanding, with ourselves and our purpose in this lifetime, and with all beings—sustained through a deep knowing and acceptance that *We Are One.*

A healed heart is an open heart that has weathered storms; a heart that has been broken and that through its cracks, invites the healing light of Love in and allows its Loving light to shine out; a heart that continues to be nourished through Love, gratitude, acceptance, and ongoing courageous acts of forgiveness and letting go.

Thinking about a healed heart reminds of the five-hundred-year-old Japanese art of kintsugi or "golden joinery," which is a method of restoring broken pottery with a lacquer that is mixed with gold, platinum, or silver. Kintsugi is interwoven with the philosophy of *wabi sabi*, which means "to find beauty in broken things."

Unlike the general Western point of view that broken objects have lost their value, the kintsugi method conveys a philosophy not of replacement, but of awe, reverence, and restoration. The gold-filled cracks of a once-broken object restore, not necessarily the physical beauty of the object, but rather its inherent value, which continues to be honored.

You may be applying this philosophy whenever you recycle, repurpose, and reincarnate an object that would otherwise be cast aside or thrown away.

So it is with heart healing; there is an acknowledgment that there have been wounds and pain in our lives, accompanied by the seemingly rational desire to close our hearts to protect ourselves, both now and in the future, from feeling the emotional, spiritual, and physical pain of the horrors of abuse, violence, and betrayals, as well as the debilitating shame and guilt of harming others through our thoughts, words, and actions.

Ironically, by armoring our hearts and placing conditions on expressing our Love, we close ourselves to the wisdom, joy, compassion, kindness, and power of Love in our lives. We allow the wounds of the past to dominate our present, unaware that until our hearts are healed, we will continue to experience life through the filter of our wounds and the beliefs we have that Love hurts.

I realize now that my heart healing journey began long before the question I wrote in my journal at fourteen years old: 'What would the world be like if everyone loved themselves?' Here's the story that makes the most sense to me right now, and I have seen it play over and over again in my life and with family, friends, and clients:

Just as an acorn has within it the potential to be a mighty oak tree, each of us is born with the potential to be a mighty expression of Love in the world—with our Love reflected in different ways dependent on our particular combination of gifts, talents, and skills.

As we grow, develop, and learn about life on Earth from the significant authority figures in our lives (parents, siblings, friends, teachers, the media, and more), we unconsciously assimilate their beliefs and points of view about life, including who to trust and who not to trust—who to Love and who not to Love. In this way, personal, cultural, generational, and current biases perpetuate in our points of view about ourselves, love, sex, religion, race, and all the -isms that separate and divide people within themselves, their families, workplaces, communities, and the world.

Unfortunately, even though the age-old wisdom that "We are One" is espoused in the spiritual foundations of every major religion of the world (since every religion has its version of the Golden Rule, "Do unto others as you would have them do unto you"), large segments of the population continue to blame and violently abuse others, from sibling rivalry in families to the ethnic cleansing that continues in parts of the world today.

Courageously opening our hearts and minds to the beliefs that generate our misery and suffering is the starting point of our healing. Just as when we use a GPS to get to where we want to go, we must start with our current location. We can only experience greater Love in our life by starting where we are—with what is. We must feel the feelings—the unworthiness, "I'm not enough-ness," victimization, shame, guilt, anger, desire for revenge, and hopelessness—that block the flow of Love to become beacons of Love and light in our personal lives and in the larger world we inhabit. It is through the practice of forgiveness of ourselves and others that we continually deepen and expand our capacity to truly give and receive Love.

If you are plagued by a current heartbreak and wounds of the past, heart healing offers you freedom—the freedom to open your heart and mind to greater Love, happiness, and appreciation of the gifts of your one wild and precious life.

●

CONCEPT 3: WHY HEART HEALING NOW?

The greatest challenge of the day is: how to bring about a revolution of the heart, a revolution which has to start with each one of us.
—Dorothy Day

Why start heart healing now? Here's the quick answer, if you are interested in greater personal happiness, fulfillment, peace of mind, and Love in your life, then now is always a good time for heart healing.

At the same time, there is a loud and deep call for heart healing—for Love—throughout the planet right now. According to the Gun Violence Archive, between January and mid-June, 2018, there were a total of 26,557 incidences of gun violence in the United States. Also, the polarization across racial, ethnic, religious, gender, sexual preference, and political lines continues to fuel wars, genocide, terrorist acts, abuse, and an "us vs. them" point of view that blocks a deep knowing that it is our diversity that adds richness to our lives.

The often spoken message from President Trump to "Make America Great Again" speaks of a time when life, liberty, and the pursuit of happiness were not applied to all people in the United States—rather to a time when people of color, women, and indigenous people, as well as people identifying as LGBTQ, were not afforded the same rights as privileged white skinned citizens, in particular, white males.

At a time when the call for peace and acceptance echoes throughout the land, the dark shadow of hatred, blame, bullying, and the desire for revenge—evidence of individual as well as collective broken hearts—appears to take center stage in the media.

As I am bombarded with news stories of all that is wrong in the world at any hour of day or night, I am reminded of a lecture I attended at the 92nd Street Y in New York City about sixteen years ago. Karen Armstrong is a British author and commentator known for her books on comparative religion, as well as the creator of the Charter for Compassion (crafted by a group of leading inspirational thinkers from the three Abrahamic traditions of Judaism, Christianity, and Islam and based on the fundamental principles of universal justice and respect).

A few years earlier, I had attempted to read her book, *The History of God: The 4,000 Year Quest of Judaism, Christianity and Islam*. It was too dense for me, so needless to say, I hoped I could follow her talk. Not only was I able to follow it, but now, more than a decade later, it still offers me a perspective that allows me to keep my heart open in the midst of the great divides of fear, hatred, bigotry, and misogyny so evident in the world today.

I recall her saying that when we take the long view of history, we see that whenever there is a major paradigm shift in our worldview, there is a rise of fundamentalism, a deep desire to return a time that in retrospect, is known and familiar compared to the disconcerting uncertainty of a new age. This is also true in our personal lives when we are in the midst of major change (even a desired, chosen change); there comes a point when we yearn to hold onto an idealized past and demonize those who are at the forefront of the new age.

We are in the midst of just this kind of paradigm shift today. Fundamentalism, extreme conservatism, and nationalism have surfaced. In this "us vs. them" arena, there is the notion that those who do not agree with these extreme beliefs are less human and therefore do not deserve equal rights to life, liberty, and the pursuit of happiness.

If you are reading this page, I imagine that the call for heart healing is something that has captured your attention. Whether globally or personally, I have found it quite useful to be aware of the paradigm shift we are currently experiencing on a global scale. It offers a framework to set us on our heart healing path.

•

CONCEPT 4: OLD & NEW PARADIGM

Paradigm (pair-uh-dahym) a cognitive framework shared by members of any discipline or group containing basic assumptions and ways of thinking.
—Dictionary.com

- **Old:** Man is born into sin and is essentially corrupt at the core
- **New:** All people in their core essence are beautiful and worthy of love.

- **Old:** Hatred and vengeance are justified for wrongs suffered—an eye for an eye.
- **New:** Love is the most transformative force. Forgiveness is an act of courage and compassion.

- **Old:** Don't show real feelings, or you'll get hurt. Create a convincing persona to present to the world.
- **New:** Welcome authenticity and vulnerability. It's all about being honest and real with ourselves and one another.

- **Old:** Emphasis on hierarchies. Focus on competition so that the best rise to the top of the hierarchy.
- **New:** Emphasis on equality. Focus on cooperation to support the greatest good for all.

- **Old:** Avoid personal responsibility by blaming those above or below you in the hierarchy.

- **New:** Take personal responsibility for our actions and learn from our mistakes.

- **Old:** People need to be led or controlled by those believed to be better or more capable.
- **New:** Each individual is a powerful creator capable of meeting their needs with the help of others.

- **Old:** The mind and science are supreme. The scientific paradigm supersedes God and religion.
- **New:** The sacred union of heart and mind and personal relationships are of paramount importance. The deepest essence of life is a divine mystery to be welcomed and explored.

- **Old:** Don't question the accepted scientific paradigm. Focus on the three-dimensional world of the five senses.
- **New:** Foster fluid intelligence. Explore the edges of consciousness, especially other dimensions and capabilities not believed to be possible under the old paradigm.

- **Old:** Categorizing and dissecting nature allows us to better control it and to profit from it.
- **New:** Recognizing the interconnectedness of all life leads to greater growth and harmony.

- **Old:** Focus on order and discipline.
- **New:** Welcome flexibility, disorder, and even occasional chaos as means to seeing new possibilities.

- **Old:** Value boundaries, borders, and divisions. These give security, safety, and comfort.

- **New:** While respecting and honoring differences, look for shared visions and ways to work together. Take risks to grow.

- **Old:** You can't trust anyone.
- **New:** Surrender to and trust in a divine power greater than our ego-oriented selves.

- **Old:** Focus on defeating and conquering the enemy; "us versus them." Make war against evil.
- **New:** Commit to transforming and integrating life's challenges. See the external world as a reflection of our inner world.

- **Old:** Focus on details and complexity.
- **New:** Remember the bigger picture. Identify simple principles behind the complexities of life.

- **Old:** Look outwards for guidance. Don't trust self. Have rigid rules and beliefs.
- **New:** Look inwards and outwards for guidance. Develop intuition and flexible guidelines and beliefs.

•

CONCEPT 5: THE TOOLS OF HEART HEALING

Please forgive me.
I forgive you.
Thank you.
I love you.
These four simple statements are powerful tools for
improving your relationships and your life.
—Dr. Ira Byock, from *The Four Things that Matter Most*

There are many exercises, techniques, and practices that fuel heart healing (many of which are in my book, *The Wholehearted Life: Big Changes and Greater Happiness Week by Week*). I have chosen to focus on the undeniable life-changing power of forgiveness in this book, both because of its potent ripple effect in healing my heart and because of the transformations I have seen in thousands of clients when they have said *Yes* to being forgiving and letting go of their attachment to their beliefs that continue to activate wounds of the past.

Before we begin a detailed exploration of using forgiveness to heal heartbreak, let's take a look at research that has been done focusing on the impact of forgiveness and unforgiveness. In his article, "The New Science of Forgiveness," Everett L. Worthington, Commonwealth Professor at Virginia Commonwealth University, reports that the practice of forgiveness carries tremendous health benefits:

> *"Forgiveness isn't just practiced by saints and martyrs, nor does it benefit only its recipients. Instead, studies are finding connections between forgiveness and physical, mental, and spiritual health, and evidence that it*

plays a key role in the health of families, communities, and nations. Though this research is still young, it has already produced some exciting findings."

Worthington cites a study by Charlotte vanOyen Witvliet, a psychologist at Hope College, who:

"...asked people to think about someone who had hurt, mistreated, or offended them. While they thought about this person and his or her past offense, she monitored their blood pressure, heart rate, facial muscle tension, and sweat gland activity. To ruminate on an old transgression is to practice unforgiveness. Sure enough, in Witvliet's research, when people recalled a grudge, their physical arousal soared. Their blood pressure and heart rate increased, and they sweated more. Ruminating about their grudges was stressful, and subjects found the rumination unpleasant. It made them feel angry, sad, anxious, and less in control. Witvliet also asked her subjects to try to empathize with their offenders or imagine forgiving them. When they practiced forgiveness, their physical arousal coasted downward. They showed no more of a stress reaction than normal wakefulness produces."

The article continues with the work of British researchers Peter Woodruff and Tom Farrow:

"Their research suggests that the areas in the brain associated with forgiveness are often deep in the emotional centers, in the region known as the limbic system, rather than in the areas of the cortex usually associated with reasoned judgments. In one study, they asked people to judge the fairness of a transgression and then consider whether to forgive it or empathize with the transgressor. Ten individuals evaluated several social scenarios while the researchers recorded images of their brain activity. Whether people empathized or forgave, similar areas in the emotion centers of the brain lit up. When those same people thought about the fairness of the same transgression,

though, the emotion centers stopped being as active. This could be a clue for interventionists. To help people forgive, help them steer clear of dwelling on how fair a transgression was or how just a solution might be. Instead, get people to see things from the other person's perspective."

Professor Worthington concludes his article with the following:

"Conflicts and transgressions seem inevitable as humans rub against each other. The sharp corners of our personalities irritate and scruff against those with whom we interact on a daily basis. But if the new science of forgiveness has proven anything, it's that these offenses don't need to condemn us to a life of hurt and aggravation. For years, political and religious figures such as Nelson Mandela and Archbishop Desmond Tutu in South Africa demonstrated the beauty and effectiveness of forgiveness in action. Through a harmony of research and practice, I trust that we can continue to foster forgiveness—and continue to study the effect scientifically—to bring health to individuals, relationships, and societies as a whole."

●

CONCEPT 6: WHAT IS FORGIVENESS?

Forgiveness is the journey we take toward healing
ourselves and our world.
—Desmond Tutu

Forgiveness is the act of courageously freeing our hearts and minds from the emotional and spiritual wounds that result in often repeated pain and suffering and block the flow of Love in our lives. Whether one asks for forgiveness or offers the gift of forgiveness, the result is freedom from a painful attachment to heartache. Each act of forgiveness allows you to deepen and expand your capacity to be, give, and receive Love.

Here are some quotes that capture the essence of forgiveness for me:

"To err is human; to forgive, divine."
—Alexander Pope

"None of us wants to have our life story be the sum of all the ways we have been hurt."
—From *The Book of Forgiving* by Desmond Tutu and Mpho Tutu

"Forgiving and releasing old hurts from your system is like taking a mental and emotional bath. Notice how people bathe their bodies on a regular basis, yet they will store negative, toxic junk in their mental and emotional natures for years without a cleanup."
—Doc Lew Childre, founder of the HeartMath Institute

I have found that the words of Rev. Diane Berke, founder and spiritual director of One Spirit Learning Alliance, offer a clear understanding of forgiveness:

"Forgiveness is a process by which we free ourselves from the pain and emotional bondage of holding on to hatred, bitterness, resentment, and anger; a decision to free the future from endlessly recycling the anguish of the past. To forgive is not to condone or approve of actions that are hurtful or destructive. Rather, it is the willingness to see those actions—no matter how extreme they may be—as the crying out in confusion and pain of a

human being deeply caught in fear and separation from love. And it is the understanding that the only thing that heals separation and fear is love.

To forgive means to recognize that deep within us, there is a presence of profound love, a reservoir of deep and abiding peace, that nothing outside of us can destroy or separate us from. Forgiveness is the inner choice to unite with that love and peace, and to identify with that rather than with the fear and anger in our minds. In this choice, we open to grace and become a channel for grace and healing in the world."

•

CONCEPT 7: WHAT I KNOW ABOUT FORGIVENESS

The practice of forgiveness is our most important contribution to the healing of the world.
—Marianne Williamson

• Forgiveness is an expression of Love for ourselves and ultimately, for the world.

• We forgive to heal the mental, emotional, and spiritual wounds that generate our pain and suffering.

• Asking for forgiveness is an act of courage and vulnerability.

• Offering forgiveness is an act of courage and trust.

• Forgiveness is not condoning behavior—it is openheartedly acknowledging what occurred.

• Forgiveness requires *letting go*—letting go of our attachment to the beliefs and meaning we apply to people and circumstances that continue to activate and feed past traumas and wounds.

- Forgiveness requires a perspective that sees beyond right and wrong, good and bad.

Forgiveness does not relieve someone of the responsibility for what they have done. Forgiveness does not erase accountability. It is not about turning a blind eye or even turning the other cheek. It is not about letting someone off the hook or saying it is okay to do something monstrous. Forgiveness is simply about understanding that every one of us is inherently good and inherently flawed. Within every hopeless situation and every seemingly hopeless person lies the possibility of transformation.
—Desmond Tutu

•

CONCEPT 8: WHAT ARE YOU FORGIVING?

One of the sayings in our country is Ubuntu—the essence of being human. Ubuntu speaks particularly about the fact that you can't exist as a human being in isolation. It speaks about our interconnectedness. You can't be human all by yourself, and when you have this quality— Ubuntu—you are known for your generosity.
—Desmond Tutu

Certainly, when we are forgiving or asking for forgiveness, it is for an action that resulted in pain and suffering. At the same time, it is crucial to remember that ultimately, we are forgiving ourselves and others for forgetting Divinity—the mysterious energetic life force that move through and connects all beings.

We are forgiving ourselves and others for forgetting that Love is our birthright and the choice of every one of the billions of people on the planet. Some people have not remembered this yet, so for those of us who do—like you and me—it is up to us to use the light of our Love to illuminate the path for others, out of the shadow of the darkness caused by spiritual, emotional, and mental wounds. And along the way, it is up to us to be for giving Love, compassion, and kindness.

I just reread this section and realized that there is background music playing in my mind, the children's gospel song "This Little Light of Mine" by Avis Burgeson Christiansen and Harry Dixon Loes, which I first learned in Girl Scout camp in 1958:

This little guiding light of mine
I'm gonna let it shine.
This little guiding light of mine
I'm gonna let it shine.
This little guiding light of mine
I'm gonna let it shine.
Let it shine, all the time, let it shine.

When to Forgive

When you hold resentment toward another, you are bound to that person or condition by an emotional link that is stronger than steel. Forgiveness is the only way to dissolve that link and get free.
—Catherine Ponder

Catherine Ponder's words offer a clear instruction regarding when to forgive. Consider the following questions as you read the When to Forgive Checklist:

- What steps have I already taken towards being forgiving?
- What thoughts and images pop into my mind?
- What sensations do I feel in my body?
- What am I willing to commit to forgiving?
- What am I willing to ask to be forgiven for?

In addition to any recent wounds, you may find that old traumas, shame, or hurts may surface—a memory of a time you felt abused physically, emotionally, sexually, or spiritually, or of a time when you were abusive toward yourself or another. If this occurs, write down, either in your journal, on a piece of paper, or on your computer, the emotions, and physical sensations you are feeling and the thoughts that are surfacing in your mind. The emotions that come up may include anger, fear, heartache, resentment, hopelessness, or others; and you may find yourself feeling physical sensations like sharp chest pain, headache, or stomach pain. Allow yourself to write whatever is true for you in the present moment. This is for your eyes only.

When to Forgive Checklist

- Anytime you feel resentment or regret toward yourself or another, it is time to forgive.

- When you are plagued by a circumstance from the past, it is time to forgive.

- When you believe you are right and someone else is wrong, it is time to forgive.

- When you are criticizing, blaming, and making demands of yourself and others, it is time to forgive.

- Anytime you have forgotten that all beings are an expression of the divine, it is time to forgive.

- Anytime you are anxious, afraid, or feel isolated, it is time to forgive.

- When you believe you are unworthy, not enough, or unloved, it is time to forgive.

- When misery, suffering, and complaining have taken up permanent residence in your being, it is time to forgive.

●

CONCEPT 9: SOME THOUGHTS ON LETTING GO

One of the most courageous decisions you'll ever make is to finally let go of what is hurting your heart and soul.
—Brigitte Nicole

The image I see when I think about letting go is an open hand, palm up—open to give and receive. It is easy to understand that letting go is a crucial component of forgiveness. It's not forgetting, it's not pretending something didn't occur. It is freeing our hearts and minds from the attachment to our beliefs and our point of view about a circumstance that resulted in pain, suffering, shame, vengefulness, rage, and brokenheartedness.

While thinking about letting go, I realized there is often a letting go that occurs along with the initial commitment to forgive. This is the willingness to let go of the attachment to the meaning you believe about the circumstance and the people who have caused you pain and suffering, or the willingness let go of the shame, guilt, and self-blame you experience for having harmed others through your words or action.

> **REMEMBER:** It is our attachment to our beliefs—the thoughts we have thought over and over again, charged with emotional energy—that create the stories we tell and believe about the experiences we've had.

In 1982, I learned a *Letting Go of the Strings of Attachment* visualization technique while attending a Dimensional Macrostructural Alignment (DMA®) workshop developed by Robert Fritz and Peter Senge. In the decades since, I have adapted and used it over and over again; I have made it my own and offered it to thousands of clients. (See the link for the *Cutting the Strings of Attachments* guided visualization audio recording in the Resource Section, page 191).

Cutting the Strings of Attachment Visualization

Use this guided Cutting the Strings visualization anytime you are attached to a particular person, group of people, or situation that is causing you undue stress, tension, discomfort, anxiety, or any emotions that block the flow of Love.

- Make yourself comfortable.

- Close your eyes and focus your attention on your breath; follow the path of your breath as it enters your body through your nose, circulates throughout your body, and leaves your body through your mouth.

- Easily and effortlessly focus your attention on your breath.

- If thoughts enter your mind, simply release them as you exhale and continue to focus your attention on your breath.

- Now, using the full resources of your imagination, see before you the person (or people) or circumstance that is activating your heartache, distress, anger, anxiety, and fear.

- Now become aware of your attachment to this circumstance, seeing the attachment from your body to the circumstance.

- Are you attached by a thin gossamer thread, a rope, a chain, a metal mesh cable, or perhaps a sticky spiderweb?

- Notice all the places there is an attachment from your body to this circumstance.

- Using the full resources of your imagination, with your dominant hand, reach for the perfect tool to cut off the attachment(s) as close to your body as possible.

- When you have cut every thread or string or rope or chain of attachment, see the circumstance as though it's a helium balloon, lifting up and becoming smaller and smaller as the circumstance and how it was attached to your body disappears.

- Now turn your attention to the places in your body where you cut the strings of attachment. Notice if there is still a remnant of the attachment in your body. If there is, easily and effortlessly remove it, and then release it gently to the Earth, knowing that Mother Earth has the power to transform this energetic attachment. (Do this at each spot where there was a string of attachment, if there are any.)

- You have now freed your body-mind-spirit of this attachment.

- Notice how you feel having let go of this attachment.

- Take a full cleansing deep breath, inhaling fully, exhaling completely, and at your own speed easily and effortlessly opening your eyes, wide awake, free of the attachment.

REMEMBER: While you may experience a lasting sense of freedom as a result of using this visualization, it is also possible that your beliefs and automatic, habitual emotional reactions that fuel the attachment may surface at another time—in five minutes, or the next day, month, or even years after you have used the visualization. This is not evidence that the visualization doesn't work, rather it is a reminder that you are now ready to expand your capacity to let go and open your heart to a deeper experience of Love.

Susyn's Story: The Power of Forgiveness to Heal My Broken Heart

I feel the need to preface my story by acknowledging that I have not personally experienced or perpetrated horrific acts of violence that I then forgave or for which I then asked for forgiveness. For me, this is an important reminder that any wounding experience or trauma, horrific or otherwise, constricts the flow of Love in both the perpetrator and the victim until courageous acts of forgiveness occur. This story captures my first experience with the power and magic of forgiveness.

My conscious Spiritual Journey as an adult began in 1972 when I attended a Silva Mind Control workshop. Little did I know that those two weekends would illuminate a Heart Healing path that continues to be the most magnificent adventure of my life. During this workshop, I learned that I am part of an interconnected whole of consciousness (the collective consciousness) and that I can create my reality based on where I focus my attention. Experiencing life through my ego-mind results in a sense of separation; experiencing life through my spiritual heart center results in a deep sense of connection, both within myself and with All beings.

Throughout my ever deepening and expanding Heart Healing journey, I've bumped up against the challenges of forgiving many times—sometimes gently, sometimes with heart-wrenching force. I knew it was a good idea to be forgiving. I was very practiced at saying, "I'm sorry," even at times when there wasn't anything to be sorry about. But when there was reason for me to ask to be forgiven, I was often stopped in my tracks by shame and righteousness. For many, many years—decades—I was seduced by and attached to the stories of how someone did me wrong. I was so good at weaving these stories that more often than not, even if I'd been the perpetrator of a wrongdoing, I could work it out in my mind and rationalize that there was someone else to blame! Or I would expertly blame myself, and by so doing, send my "I'm not enough-ness" and unworthiness beliefs into high gear.

I liked thinking I was forgiving, but I continued to be angry, particularly toward family members and lovers when they did not meet my expectations. While I thought I understood forgiveness as a concept, the act of truly forgiving—forgiving myself for believing that I was the victim of the thoughts and actions of others, or forgiving others for doing the best they could do at any moment based on their thinking and beliefs—was just beyond my comprehension. Then one evening in December, 1983, I had an experience with forgiveness that changed my life.

B and I had been divorced for six years when I wrote to him asking for copies of home movies we had made during our marriage. While I was curious to see all of the movies, I was particularly eager to see the ones with my dad, who had died nine years earlier.

Weeks passed, and then finally B responded, telling me that he had considered my request and decided he did not want to send me the movies. I was shocked. B was a director of a hospice program. His letter came on official hospice stationary. He was refusing to send me home movies that included my dad in the years before his death.

After a few days, it occurred to me that he might have decided not to send them because I had not included money to make copies of the movies. I wrote to him again, enclosing a check, and made sure to point out—with a snarky attitude—that since he worked as a hospice director, I thought he would understand that I wanted to see the movies of my dad. Weeks later, B's next letter echoed the sentiments of the first one: "I made movies before I met you. I've continued to make movies since we've been divorced, and I will decide who gets to see my movies." I thought, 'This guy has a problem.'

Months passed. A friend invited me to a forgiveness program at The Open Center in New York City given by Robin Casajarian, who offered forgiveness workshops in prisons. One cold December evening, we sat and listened as Robin spoke about the power of forgiveness. She led us through a guided visualization. I closed my eyes and following her instructions, cleared my focus, and directed my attention to her words: "...Notice a door on the right side of the room. In a few moments, someone will walk through that door. Forgive that person." Using the full resources of my imagination, I saw the door, and when it opened, B appeared and walked toward me, stopping directly in front of me.

With my ego-mind, I could hear myself say to him, 'I forgive you for having an affair soon after my sister died, and years later, for telling me you were in love with someone else during the time my dad was dying.' Then I heard another voice, quieter this time, but concise and direct, as though it came straight from my heart: 'I forgive you for loving me.'

I was stunned. I knew this was the profound truth beneath all the obvious reasons I had been angry with him during our marriage and at times, since our divorce. For me to have accepted his love, I had to first love myself, and I had not. Through the years of our marriage, I had projected all my self-loathing onto him. The more he loved me, the more I projected. With this realization, I felt energized, light-hearted, and as though a very important gift had been presented to me.

Ten days later, I was in New Hampshire—where B and I had lived during the last three years of our marriage. On the afternoon of New Year's Eve 1983, I was shopping in a giant supermarket when I suddenly knew B was in the store. I walked up and down a few aisles until I was standing in front him. After saying hello to one another, he asked, "Did you get the movies? I sent them to you about ten days ago."

When I truly forgave B for having an affair and not being emotionally available during deaths in my family, and even more importantly, forgave him for loving me, and ultimately forgave myself for believing that I was not worthy of love, the movies that contained loving memories of our life together were awaiting my return to NYC.

This is the way forgiveness works. When we finally let go of our attachment to the hurt, the anger, the need to be right, and the need to make others wrong, we not only release ourselves from the bonds of resentment, we also discover that the precious gifts of life find their way to us. This is the power of forgiveness. My heart opened to a more loving relationship with myself, and ultimately, this opening has deepened my commitment to live a healed-hearted and wholehearted life every day.

By the way, after the visualization at The Open Center, any open wounds or resentments that had been triggered when I thought of B dissolved. And now, thirty-five years later, it is a treat to receive birthday wishes from him and to send them his way. When he learned of the dramatic ending of my relationship with Beau, he sent me this message, "If there's anyone who can turn lemons into lemonade, it's you."

●

CONCEPT 10: FORGIVENESS IN ACTION

Have you ever heard yourself or someone else say, "It's just the way I am"? I'm a firm believer that as long as you're breathing, it's possible to upgrade the programming of your mind—your conditioning.

Our days are filled with thousands of thoughts, conscious and unconscious, and hundreds of actions, visible and invisible. Sometimes, we do our best to be compassionate and consider others when making choices; more often, we allow our thoughts and actions free rein, so they are habitual, unconscious, and an automatic reflection of our beliefs.

It is not that we are intentionally unkind and selfish; it is that we most often operate unconsciously through the filters of our limited point of view without thinking about the impact of our words and actions. As a result, someone is hurt by our words and becomes angry with us—or we become angry with ourselves for not anticipating the outcome. This is the path of least resistance. It is as though we are in a trance of automatic action leading to reaction. This is why committing to healing our hearts and living a wholehearted life is truly wake-up work—mindfulness, calling on us to be conscious in the present moment.

Other times, with our ego-mind—the part of us that separates, compares, and judges—in the driver's seat, we take actions based on lack, feeling like we need, deserve, or should have something we do not possess. Or fear compels us to take an action that is hurtful to others or ourselves. This can be an action as simple as stealing office supplies from our workplace because we did not get the raise we thought we deserved, or it can be as extreme as murdering someone because we believe they are living on land that belongs to us, or because they call G-d by a different name, or because their skin color, sexual orientation, or gender identity is different and not as "good" as ours, and we believe they are to blame for whatever problems exist.

We may also hurt others when their beliefs, opinions, and ideas challenge our notion of what is right. This can happen when a family member does not agree with our point of view and we choose to cut them out of our lives. It happens on a larger scale when one religious group does not agree with the beliefs of another group, and the groups choose to blame, terrorize, or go to war with each other.

Humans are the only species that continually engages in self-punishment by using the full resources of imagination to reexperience past wounds, traumas, and painful events. We regret something we have said or did not say, or something we have done or did not do, or we blame someone else for their actions or failure to act. Each time we remember the wounding event, we reactivate feelings of hurt, anger, sadness, and suffering. This causes distress and heartache, ultimately constricting the inflow and outflow of Love in our lives.

Forgiveness is the action of letting go and surrendering our attachment to judging circumstances from our own limited point of view. Conflict arises when people act according to their beliefs and concepts without acknowledging that other people have their own concepts and beliefs—and that all of us feel that our ideas are the ones that are the truth! In short, ignorance and judgments of another person's point of view cause suffering.

For example, if someone commits a murder, we understand that something in that person's mind compelled them to take this action. We may become very angry and feel deep hatred toward that person and judge them harshly. The solution is to see "what is" in the situation. In this case, it's that someone acted in ignorance of the true nature of humanity—that we are one—and that by hurting another, we hurt ourselves, creating suffering both in ourselves and in others. This was expressed powerfully by Jesus in Luke 23:34 when he said on the cross, "Father, forgive them; for they know not what they do."

When we find ourselves in the most challenging circumstances, our ability to transcend judgment and retaliation is put to the test. Throughout human history, we have seen situations where people who were abused and tortured have found it in their hearts to forgive those who harmed them. This may seem like an extraordinary way of thinking and acting, but I assure you that all of us can forgive and have compassion for those who hurt us, particularly when we remember that we forgive and let go to free our hearts and minds from continued misery and suffering. The following story is a powerful example of forgiving what initially seems to be impossible to forgive.

Father Forgives Son's Killer

On January 21, 1995, Tariq Khamisa, age twenty, was shot and killed by Tony Hicks, a fourteen-year-old gang member, while Tariq was delivering pizza in San Diego, CA. Tony had followed an order from an eighteen-year-old gang member to shoot Tariq.

Tariq was a great soul, wise, charismatic, good-looking, and a college student with a beautiful girlfriend he'd planned to marry, according to his father, Azim Khamisa. Initially, Azim said that it had taken all his willpower to climb out of bed after Tariq's death, but then he'd realized that the tragedy was about "victims at both ends of the gun," one being his son and the other a fourteen-year-old gang member who was a victim of society. So began his road to forgiveness.

From Murder to Forgiveness: "Azim first forgave the family of Tony Hicks and formed a friendship with Tony's grandfather and guardian, Ples Felix. Then in October 1995, Azim founded The Tariq Khamisa Foundation (TKF) in honor of his son. He founded TKF to 'stop kids from killing kids,' and Ples joined him in his dedication to ending youth violence."

They began giving talks in schools, teaching elementary, middle, and high school students about the realities of gangs, violence, revenge, and the importance of making the right choices in life. The foundation's entire curriculum is based on six key messages:

1. Violence is real and hurts us all.

2. Your actions have consequences.

3. You can make good and non-violent choices.

4. You can work toward forgiveness as opposed to seeking revenge.

5. Everyone, including you, deserves to be loved and treated well.

6. From conflict, love and unity are possible.

What began as the dream of a heartbroken father has grown into an organization with a full-time staff and AmeriCorps volunteers that offers a violence prevention curriculum and mentoring services to over 20,000 students annually. The foundation is committed to introducing students to core values of integrity, compassionate confrontation, and forgiveness, and to changing the lives of young people by empowering them to make positive choices to break the cycle of violence.

Forgiveness in action: Five years after the tragic death of his son, Azim met Tony Hicks and looked into his eyes for a very long time. He didn't see a murderer. He saw a soul much like himself. He and Tony became friends, and Azim guaranteed Tony a job at the foundation when he gets out of jail. His first parole hearing is scheduled for 2018.

Azim transformed his grief into a powerful commitment to change. "Change is urgently needed in a society where children kill children," he said.[1]

* * *

Azim Khamisa's story is just one example of the undeniable power of forgiveness and how the far-reaching impact of a tragedy can become the springboard for addressing the serious, heartbreaking problems that exist in the world today.

Just to be clear, forgiveness does not mean condoning acts of violence or physical, verbal, emotional, or sexual abuse—it simply means that we forgive actions committed in ignorance of our divinity and interconnectedness. I know this can be difficult to put into practice, and I also know that having the courage to forgive offers more to heal our hearts—and the world—than anger, hatred, blame, and acts of violence. Forgiveness transforms the energy of anger, hatred, resentment, and rage into focused Loving action for the highest good for *All*.

The Book of Forgiving by Desmond Tutu and his daughter, Mpho Tutu, is filled with stories of the power of forgiveness that resulted from the Truth and Reconciliation Commission (TRC), which was formed in South Africa after the first democratic election in 1994. Up until that time, Tutu writes:

"In apartheid South Africa, only white people could vote, earn a high-quality education, and expect advancement and opportunity. There were

---

1 Tariq Khamisa "Father Forgives Son's Killer." *Virtues for Life*.
   http://www.virtuesforlife.com/father-forgives-sons-killer/.

decades of protest and violence. Much blood was shed during our long march to freedom. When at last our leaders were released from prison, it was feared that our transition would become a bloodbath of revenge and retaliation. Miraculously, we chose another future. We chose forgiveness. At the time, we knew that telling the truth and healing our history was the only way to save our country from certain destruction. We did not know where this choice would lead us. The process we embarked on through the TRC was, as all real growth proves to be, astoundingly painful and profoundly beautiful."

•

CONCEPT 11: REVENGE OR FORGIVENESS

I must admit that while I have files, books by other authors, and even my own earlier books, that are all filled with practices, exercises, and techniques to generate Heart Healing, I know that forgiveness is undeniably the most potent tool to have in your medicine bag to ensure a healed heart. Forgiveness models make it clear that forgiveness and letting go is not a linear process that has a particular time frame. Sometimes, acts of forgiveness reap immediate and lasting heart healing, particularly when forgiveness becomes a component of your daily practice. Other times, it's like raising veil after veil after veil, healing your heart along the way, as you continually deepen and expand your capacity to be a mighty expression of Love in the world, layer by layer. Here is the story of one of my Heart Healing Coaching clients:

When our sessions began, Meredith was ready to forgive her ex-husband for divorcing her three years earlier. She was sick and tired of being filled with anger, resentment, and shame and of feeling certain that she would never be able to love and trust another and that she was doomed at thirty-two years old to be alone forever.

As I learned more about her childhood, it became clear that abandonment was a major theme and fear in her life. Meredith's parents had divorced when she was seven years old. Her father left for work one morning and never returned. While her mother was present, her shock, anger, and depression often left Meredith taking care of her mom and younger brother, another form of abandonment that strengthened her belief that she couldn't count on people who said they loved her.

When her husband told her one morning, seemingly out of the blue, that he was filing for divorce, she was convinced without a shadow of doubt that there was something wrong with her. She now had more evidence that she could not count on people who said they loved her.

During the next three years, her anger was either directed toward her ex-husband, feeding her desire for revenge, or turned inward toward herself. She began our coaching relationship with the mindset that she was committed to forgiving and letting go of the resentment she had directed toward him, and more importantly, to forgiving herself for believing that she was not lovable—that she was not worthy and deserving of love.

Three months after our coaching sessions began, she met Martin. She was excited about getting to know him, and he was eager to spend more and more time with her. After dating for two months, he told her that he had fallen in love with her. As much as she had yearned to hear those words said, she immediately became fearful that as he continued to spend time with her, he would discover that she wasn't worthy of his love and that he would leave her, just like the other men in her life.

She was furious when she came to our next coaching session—her fears had come to life. The day before, she'd had dinner plans with Martin. They had arranged to meet at 7:00 p.m. at her favorite restaurant. Martin had texted her earlier in the day saying, "Eager 2 c u 2nite @ 7pm @ restaurant. B with clients all day. C u later. ♥ *"*

Throughout the day, Meredith was excited about seeing Martin. She felt beautiful as she drove to the restaurant. She arrived a few minutes early and was seated at a table where she would see Martin as soon as he arrived. Five minutes, ten minutes, and then fifteen minutes passed, and no Martin. She texted him; no response. She called him; no response. After twenty-five minutes sitting alone at a table for two, feeling hyperaware of all the couples enjoying dinner together, she snuck out of the restaurant, certain that Martin was like every other man she had ever met and furious at herself for having thought that he loved her.

Although Martin had called and texted her repeatedly between 9:00 p.m. the night before and today, the day of our session, she had deleted all of the messages. She was through with him and had no intention of ever talking with him again, since he was clearly like every other man she had ever cared for—like every other man who had ever said he loved her.

When she had finished her tearful emotional story of being stood up, I asked, "Is it possible that the meaning you are giving to last night's experience with Martin is based on your personal history? Maybe there is another explanation." Her response was immediate and defensive, "How can there be another explanation? He told me he loved me last Saturday, and now four days later, he stood me up. I think it's pretty clear I can't trust him."

By the end of the session, Meredith said, "Well, he did call and text me many, many times, and he sent me a beautiful bouquet with a note that read, 'I'm sorry about last night. I Love You. Please give me a chance to explain.' Without skipping a beat. Meredith said, "I guess I could at least hear what he has to say. Maybe I have been a prisoner of that old belief that I'm not worthy and deserving of love."

Two hours later, Meredith called me. Excitedly, she told me that she had forgiven Martin and proceeded to tell me what had happened: "Martin had stopped home after work for a quick shower. He left the house and *realized that he'd forgotten his phone, and he was so eager to be with me and not keep me waiting that he didn't go back to the house to get it. Along the way, he got a flat tire and didn't have a spare. Without a phone, he couldn't call me or roadside service. He walked a half mile to a gas station to get assistance and then realized that he couldn't call me, since he hadn't memorized my phone number, which was in his phone. He called the restaurant, but I'd already left. By the time he got home, it was 9:00 p.m. That is when he started calling me. He even said that if I thought this was a far-fetched excuse for standing me up, that he'd show me the tow truck receipt. He's on his way over here now, to take me out to dinner."*

While Meredith still had to give attention to forgiving and letting go of the pain of her divorce, she was able to see that her beliefs about not being worthy and deserving of Love had served as a filter through which she then made meaning out of her experience of Martin not showing up when expected. Her vulnerability in sharing her experience with me and her willingness to consider that her assumptions about Martin and the previous evening might not be accurate allowed her to forgive him and loosen the hold on her self-sabotaging beliefs.

After a year and a half of Heart Healing Coaching, Meredith forgave herself completely for believing that she was unworthy and undeserving of being loved and opened herself wholeheartedly to Love.

•

CONCEPT 12: A FORGIVENESS ROADMAP

Even with ready access to an abundance of resources, I found myself stuck for months while wanting to create the perfect map for Heart Healing—a GPS that would allow you to discover where you are and identify healing steps, tasks, and road signs along the way. I sat facing the blank screen of my computer, eager to see the words for a simple to understand and useful model for forgiveness and letting go. Minute by minute, I became more frustrated with the process, as my ego-mind was attached to developing the best, most important model ever seen. As my frustration grew, my judgments about myself and writing this book surfaced. I heard these words echoing through my mind: 'You have some forgiving and letting go to do here, Susyn. You have just spent the last twenty-five minutes judging and criticizing yourself.' I immediately began to laugh aloud!

In my desire to immediately devise the best forgiveness model to use, I had begun to feel and believe that I was not enough— not smart enough, wise enough, nor intelligent enough. It was my ability to laugh at myself that pulled me through—you know those uncontrollable spontaneous belly laughs. It was as though I had just gotten the cosmic joke of the situation—a joke that resulted in my knowing that my value as a human being is not based on my developing the best forgiveness map on the planet! I forgave myself for the judgments I'd made and immediately placed my hands on my heart, closed my eyes, and declared to G-d, the Loving Energy of the Universe, "I'm ready to know the best model of forgiveness and letting go for the readers of this book. Show me."

I opened my eyes and noticed the stack of forgiveness books and articles on the floor beside my desk, resources that I had forgotten about. I spent the next couple of hours reading and realized that the Revenge Cycle and Forgiveness Cycle described in *The Book of Forgiving* by Desmond and Mpho Tutu speaks most powerfully to me.

The Revenge Cycle: For both the Revenge and Forgiveness Cycles, the starting point is an action that causes suffering, hurt, harm, or loss—an Ouch. In the Revenge Cycle, the choice is To Harm, leading to:

Rejecting Shared Humanity—we are not one; you are other

↓

Revenge, Retaliation, Payback—desire to hurt or harm the perpetrator

↓

Violence—the act of revenge

↓

Hurt, Harm, and Loss

...and the cycle continues.

A deeper look at the Revenge Cycle: There is an action of violence, cruelty, betrayal, or abuse that occurs that results in pain, hurt, and loss. If the choice to harm in return is made, retaliation leads to further violence and pain, and so the cycle continues on, not unlike conflicts that continue today, whether within ourselves, families, communities, and nations.

In the Revenge Cycle, instead of focusing on healing the hurt and pain of our broken hearts and moving on with our lives, in order to restore our dignity, we seem compelled to continually focus our attention on the perpetrator; by so doing and by choosing revenge as the path to justice, we fail to acknowledge our shared humanity.

REMEMBER: The choice to retaliate is an indicator that you have embarked on the Revenge Cycle. This is not something to judge yourself about; it simply lets you know that you believe that revenge and retaliation are the paths to healing your heart. The Revenge Cycle is a perfect description of the old paradigm of an eye for an eye—which can leave everyone blind!

Consider the following questions:

- Is the Revenge Cycle alive in your life? Towards whom?

- Do you see patterns in your relationships of this cycle being enacted over and over again? This is so easy to see with children when one says, "But I didn't start it." There comes a point where it doesn't matter who started it; the revenge, retaliation, and payback pattern has begun.

- How many conflicts, acts of terror, and wars are age-old continuations of the Revenge Cycle?

The Forgiveness Cycle: Forgiveness begins with the choice To Heal after the Ouch of an act of violence or cruelty that resulted in hurt, harm, or loss. Making this choice opens the way to:

Telling the Story and Naming the Hurt—what happened and its impact on you physically, emotionally, and spiritually

↓

Granting Forgiveness—opening your heart to your shared humanity

↓

Renewing or Releasing the Relationship—free of the wound of the past

↓

A Healed Heart—open to give and receive Love

Here's a deeper look at each component of the Forgiveness Cycle: Telling the Story and Naming the Hurt begins with the willingness to be specific about "what is" the trauma you've experienced. It is not important to tell it in chronological order, and the telling may be fragmented and difficult to express. It is the choice to honestly, vulnerably, and authentically tell the story that initiates the forgiveness cycle. I often think of this as being like a GPS; to arrive at your healed heart desired destination, you must be clear and specific about where you are starting, which is your current situation. Telling the story includes naming the hurt, expressing your feelings, and the impact of this hurt on your life and the lives of those others touched by the cruelty.

To whom do you tell the story? Sometimes, the starting place is in your journal, where you feel safe to express yourself free from the reactions, opinions, and judgments of others. There are times when shame clouds our ability and courage to share our story with another, so our journals may then become our trusted ally on the path to healing our hearts.

In her book *Writing Down Your Soul: How to Activate and Listen to the Extraordinary Voice Within*, Janet Conner shares her forgiveness story; it began with the daily practice of writing down her soul. She writes, "I was a busy woman—a woman with no time to journal."

This all changed on November 1, 1996. The summer before, Janet had caught her husband sleeping with his secretary. Though he moved out that September, he had not moved on. On Halloween, her seven-year-old-son begged her to invite his dad for their annual extravaganza. He joined them, but after trick-or-treating, her ex would not leave the house and demanded they have sex—and when she refused, he shoved her out the door.

Janet continues, *"He screamed that I'd never see my child again. He drank. He broke furniture. He cried. He drank some more. When he finally left at one in the morning, I collapsed into a dense, dark sleep. At dawn, my eyes shot open, five words rocketing to the surface: I am afraid of you. Those words changed my life. I called my husband at noon and told him I wanted a divorce."*

While there is more to Janet's story, the traumatic Halloween incident set her on the path to writing down her soul—daily written conversations with God. When she was asked to speak about forgiveness at a local church three years later, to prepare, she went to her journal and wrote, "Dear God, I don't have enough material on forgiveness, and you know all about it! OK, I get it: the teacher needs to teach what the teacher needs to learn. Well, I'm ready. I just don't know how to do it. You show me how to forgive, and I will forgive."

This led to her forgiving her former husband, healing her heart, and having him over for dinner twice a week for fifteen months until his death on October 6, 2003.

As valuable as it is to have your journal as your confidant and fill its pages with what is most deeply personal and heartfelt, sharing your story with another person or group generally elicits unexpected support and encouragement that dissolves the closed-hearted isolation of unexpressed pain. The courage to be vulnerable and authentically share your experience is a potent antidote for the shame or survivor's guilt that victims of loss often feel. Telling the story is equally important for the perpetrator of abuse and cruelty. Telling the story to others is an act of courage since reliving the experience through openheartedly sharing reactivates the pain associated with the event, even long after it has occurred. It is in this telling that feelings that have been locked away—sometimes for decades—are released and transformed.

REMEMBER: Unpacking an old wound often activates very strong reactions—physically, mentally, emotionally, and spiritually. When in the throes of this kind of suffering, seeking professional guidance and support is a potent reflection of your commitment to forgive, let go, and heal your broken heart.

When I started leading personal development groups in the mid-1970s, I came across these words by Carl R. Rogers, an American psychologist and proponent of client-centered therapy and unconditional positive regard, "What is most personal is most universal." This idea gave me the courage to be vulnerable and share my most heartfelt feelings. As I authentically spoke about my "not enough-ness" as well as my gifts, talents, and skills, I discovered that while our personal experiences and circumstances are different, the range of human emotions we experience are the same. With this in mind, I encourage myself, family, friends, and clients to share their wounds—their shadows—authentically. It is this vulnerability that is an act of Love.

REMEMBER: While speaking your truth with others is important, you must make a conscious choice regarding with whom you share your story. Your goal of being vulnerable in sharing your story is to free your heart and mind of pain and suffering, poor self-esteem, and feelings of unworthiness, not to gather support to take actions that are fueled by the desire for revenge.

Follow these guidelines for telling your story:

- Consciously choose who to tell your story to—a trusted family member, friend, loved one, therapist, coach, or clergyperson.

- Be honest.

- Start with "what is"—describing the circumstance.

- Tell the impact this experience has had on you, physically, mentally (your thoughts), emotionally, and spiritually.

- Consider telling your story to the person who harmed you or the person you harmed. Writing a letter, whether or not you send it, is a powerful starting point.

- Accept that the situation occurred and cannot be changed.

Follow these guidelines when listening to the story to demonstrate unconditional positive regard and create a safe space for the speaker:

- Focus your attention on the speaker. (If you do not have the time to listen or if the topic is too emotionally charged for you, communicate this directly.)

- Ask how you can be helpful and supportive (for example, by asking, "What would be most helpful for you, for me to listen; to tell you what I heard you say; to share how I would handle the situation; or to play the devil's advocate and present a different point of view...?)

- Accept the speaker's story as true for them.

- Do not cross-examine the speaker—you are here to listen and provide the support requested by the speaker.

- Do not take the attention away from the speaker by sharing your experiences; remember you are a witness and listener.

- Acknowledge what happened and its impact on the speaker (paraphrase what you've heard).

- Acknowledge the feelings the speaker expresses.

- Acknowledge the speaker for their willingness and courage in sharing their story.

Granting Forgiveness—Recognizing Shared Humanity: When the story is told and deeply listened to, there is the possibility for magic to occur. This is the precious gift of being courageously vulnerable and honest when telling your story. Through open hearted communication between the forgiver and the forgiven, an energetic connection is forged that recognizes shared humanity.

Renewing or Releasing the Relationship: Once forgiveness has been granted, there is the choice to renew or release the relationship. You are not a good person if you renew the relationship, nor are you a bad person if you release it. I have found that the best way for me to make this decision if I'm unsure is to ask the wisdom of my heart, "What would Love do here?"

A Healed Heart—Living a Wholehearted Life: Living a wholehearted life is sustained by a daily practice that nourishes your body, mind, and spirit. It is not only the food you feed your body and the physical exercise you practice, it also includes the thoughts you think and your daily connection with the Loving Energy of the Universe. And of course, it also includes a daily forgiveness check—forgiving yourself and others so wounds don't turn into scars that block the flow of Love.

●

CONCEPT 13: COMMIT FIRST

When I have forgiven myself and remembered who I Am,
I will bless everyone and everything I see.
—Helen Schucman, *A Course in Miracles*

Ultimately, this book is an invitation and a challenge to you to move past judgment itself—otherwise, we are continually judging, criticizing, and condemning ourselves and others. This is where we get stuck over and over again, in constantly judging, becoming angry, and then having to forgive. When we take full responsibility for ourselves and learn to see ourselves and each other as divine beings, we not only heal our hearts, we cross the threshold to heaven on earth.

Our commitments are that which we orbit around. They
are our sun, and they feed us the ability to organize our
lives around that which is meaningful to us.
—Katherine Woodward Thomas

Often, we wait to commit until we are certain that all the i's are dotted, all the t's are crossed, and our desired result is guaranteed. We hesitate to commit too soon, filled with fearful thoughts: 'What if this doesn't work out? What if I can't do this?'

Have you ever noticed that fear and anxiety often go into overdrive when you are faced with taking a stand and making a commitment? This can occur independent of the magnitude of the specific choice being made—whether it's getting married, ending a relationship, becoming a parent, running for a political office, leaving your successful career to start your own business, going off on a travel adventure, or making a New Year's resolution to be organized, eat organic food, exercise, or meditate regularly.

When consumed by fear, do you all too often give up on your dream and allow your commitment to fear to take over? This prevents you from truly committing to your hearts' desire.

The reality of the creative process requires that you commit first. It is your commitment to your dream, to the song of your heart, that ultimately allows you to face your fears and make choices that nourish wholehearted living.

The words of W. H. Murray, a member of the 1951 Scottish Himalayan Expedition, beautifully describe the power of committing first:

> *Until one is committed, there is hesitancy, the chance to draw back, always ineffectiveness. Concerning all acts of initiative (and creation), there is one elementary truth the ignorance of which kills countless ideas and splendid plans: that the moment one commits oneself, then providence moves too. A whole stream of events issue from the decision, raising in one's favor all manner of unforeseen incidents, meetings, and material assistance which no man could have dreamt would have come his way. I learned a deep respect for one of Goethe's couplets: "Whatever you can do, or dream you can, begin it. Boldness has genius, power, and magic in it!"*

TIME TO COMMIT

To begin a journey, it is necessary to have a destination—a dream in mind. It's not necessary to know all the steps along the way; however, we do need to know where we are headed. Demonstrate your commitment to healing your heart by completing the following exercise.

Either on a piece of paper, in your journal, in the space below, or on your computer, write your responses to the following items to articulate and give voice to your commitment and faith in the undeniable power of forgiveness to heal your heart:

My dream, vision, intention, and goal in saying *yes* to Heart Healing through the undeniable power of forgiveness is: _____

_____

_____

_____

_____

_____

_____

_____

_____

_____

_____

_____

_____

_____

_____

_____

_____

My definition of forgiveness is: _____

_____

_____

_____

_____

_____
_____
_____
_____
_____
_____
_____
_____
_____
_____
_____
_____
_____
_____
_____
_____

Describe your most powerful forgiveness experience: _____

_____
_____
_____
_____
_____
_____
_____
_____
_____
_____
_____
_____

_____

_____

_____

_____

_____

_____

_____

_____

My greatest challenges to being forgiving, which I am ready and willing to transform, are: _____

_____

_____

_____

_____

_____

_____

_____

_____

_____

_____

_____

_____

_____

_____

_____

_____

_____

_____

PART III:
PRACTICING FORGIVENESS

INTRODUCTION

Since the practice of forgiveness is essential for healing a broken heart, in Part III, we explore the life-changing power of forgiveness. This section focuses on:

- Forgiving yourself
- Forgiving your body
- Forgiving your family
- Forgiving relationships

Each lesson includes an inspiring quote, practices, and a "Love Note" to yourself.

> **REMEMBER:** Feelings of victimization, resentment, shame, guilt, blame, the desire for revenge, unworthiness, and "I'm not enoughness" is an invitation for forgiveness with the promise of heart healing.

Forgive Yourself

I am often asked, "Where do I begin forgiving, who do I forgive first?" My answer is always the same, "Start by forgiving yourself." This is the starting place, since our relationship with ourselves forms the blueprint for all the relationships in our life.

Bring it up, make amends, and forgive yourself. It sounds simple, but don't think for a second that it is easy. Getting free from the tyranny of past mistakes can be hard work, but [is] definitely worth the effort. And the payoff is health, wholeness, and inner peace. In other words, you get your life back.
—Steve Goodier

•

LESSON 1: FROM SELF-SABOTAGE TO INTUITION

The mind can assert anything and pretend it has proved it. My beliefs I test on my body, on my intuitional consciousness, and when I get a response there, then I accept.
—D.H. Lawrence

Our lives are filled with choices: what to eat, what to wear, who to marry, what medical advice to follow, where to invest our money, and what political action to take. Numerous daily life choices are made automatically based on habitual thoughts and actions (automatically turning on the coffee pot in the morning, brushing your teeth, the route you take to work, school, or the market, etc.). Our bigger life choices are often influenced by the opinions, ideas, and beliefs of others, including our parents, friends, the media, and the prevailing consciousness of our culture. We look outside of ourselves for the right answer that will result in living happily ever after.

How many times in your life have you made a decision only to say afterward, I should have taken the other job; moved into the other neighborhood; or turned down another street on my way to work. I knew what to do; I had a gut feeling, I just didn't pay attention to it. It didn't seem logical! Although we may gather the opinions of others to figure out the best course of action, time after time, we fail to access our most valuable source of information—our intuition, the wisdom of our heart. We fail to acknowledge that we are wired from the inside out with a fail-safe system which, when followed, illuminates a path that nourishes our deepest desires, our greatest well-being, and is seamlessly aligned with our purpose and passion.

Take a moment to identify when you've sabotaged yourself by allowing your mind to edit what's possible for you in life. How often have you made choices and taken actions dictated by the fear-based voice of your ego-mind?

After years of muting our intuition, how do we discern between our ego-mind and our inner knowledge? The answer is simple: listen to your body.

REMEMBER: Our intuition expresses itself through our bodies as a sense of absolute knowing that may be experienced as chills, a whoosh of sensation, or amplified sensory experiences. The words that follow are simple, direct statements: make a left turn, write about forgiveness, buy this house. There's no story, no long explanation or rationale. Keep in mind that our ego-mind is our rational and linear self that separates, judges, and evaluates. It offers explanations about why its point of view is "right." To strengthen your intuition, clear the slate and forgive the ways you've sabotaged yourself in the past.

PRACTICING THE LESSON

1. What stops you from allowing your inner knowledge to direct your actions and life choices?

2. How do you experience your intuition in your body?

3. Make a list of all the choices you regret in which fear-based beliefs sabotaged your intuition.

   – Go through the list one by one and say aloud: I forgive myself for believing I made the wrong choice about _____ _____(state the item on your list).

   – Repeat this exercise for each item on your list. You may have to repeat this exercise multiple times for each item to let go.

   – Anytime you feel regret or remorse for a choice you've made, use this technique to forgive yourself.

4. When you have an important choice to make, ask yourself: What is my next step regarding _____ ? Listen to your intuition; pay attention to the sensations you are feeling in your body. Take action; follow your inner wisdom. When you trust your inner knowing, you don't have to know each step along the way; you simply follow your guidance system, discerning between the voice of your ego-mind and your inner guidance—the still small voice within. Reflect on your experience with this exercise.

LOVE NOTE TO MYSELF

I forgive myself for failing to use my intuition as my GPS. I ask for, listen to, and follow my intuition, the wisdom of my heart, to guide my choices.

•

LESSON 2: FROM JUDGMENT TO ACCEPTANCE

Whoever undertakes to set himself up as a judge of
Truth and Knowledge is shipwrecked by the laughter of
the gods.
—Edmund Burke, On Empire, Liberty, and Reform:
Speeches and Letters, 1794

How often during a day do you find yourself judging, criticizing, and evaluating yourself and others? Do you defend your judgments about others because you believe you are right? How often do you disregard another point of view because you self-righteously believe that your view is more loving, more caring, and absolutely the truth?

Our thoughts form the basis of the world we experience. When the main focus of our thinking is on what's wrong with someone else or ourselves, we're instructing our eyes only to see what is wrong, what doesn't work, or problems. Imagine your judgments and criticisms are invisible poisonous darts aimed directly at the person being judged. At the same time you are thinking these thoughts, the very poison you are projecting is moving through your very own body.

We live in an interdependent world on planet Earth. To survive and thrive, we're dependent on being in community. Communities fail when there is constant judgment and criticism of their members. Communities thrive when the worthiness, diversity, and interconnectedness of their members is acknowledged and appreciated.

Isn't it time to free ourselves from the tyranny of judging and see the perfection of each moment through the eyes of Love?

PRACTICING THE LESSON

1. Tally Up Your Judgments Challenge: For three days, pay attention to your thoughts and words from the time you get up in the morning until you fall asleep at night. When you notice you've made a judgment (this is good, that is bad; this is right, that is wrong— remember to track positive judgments as well) about yourself, others, or a situation, put a penny, quarter, dollar, paperclip, or toothpick (you choose) in a bowl. What did you discover when you tracked how many judgments you made in three days?

2. Whenever you notice you are judging yourself or others, **stop** immediately, acknowledge yourself for noticing, and say the following: "Thank you, voice of judgment, for giving me the opportunity to choose acceptance."

3. When you notice you are defending your point of view because you are "right," experiment with taking another point of view as a way to playfully expand your consciousness. Remember, a point of view is simply a made-up idea. What are the points of view you defend? What makes you believe your point of view is any more than "your truth"?

LOVE NOTE TO MYSELF

My judgments are wake-up calls to ask myself, "What would Love do here?" After doing this, listen to the response and follow the wisdom.

•

LESSON 3: FROM VICTIMHOOD TO DIVINITY

The best years of your life are the ones in which you decide your problems are your own. You don't blame them on your mother, the ecology, or the president. You realize that you control your destiny.
—Albert Ellis

Our society loves to blame. Where does this tendency come from, and why is our culture so invested in this victim mentality? When we see ourselves as victims, we don't have to take responsibility for our actions and choices. It's much easier to blame things on others—that way we don't have to feel guilty about anything.

Guilt, shame, and remorse are great strategies of the ego-mind to keep us disempowered, weak, and at the mercy of beliefs that aren't the truth. They keep us from embracing our divine nature and the power we have been given to create our reality through our thoughts, charged with emotional energy, spoken of with authority, and acted on with conviction—with faith. Most importantly, guilt, shame, and remorse allow us to abdicate the responsibility we have as co-creative partners with the Loving Energy of the Universe.

It is through awareness of our beliefs that we can see how we perpetuate heartache and suffering in our lives or the lives of others. This awareness opens the door to asking for forgiveness, forgiving ourselves, and choosing to take different actions in the future. This is called learning from our life experiences, and the lessons learned are far more valuable than feeling bad about choices we have made in the past, beating ourselves up, and becoming weighed down with guilt and shame.

PRACTICING THE LESSON

1. List three situations when you felt victimized. For each one, write down why you felt victimized. Look carefully at what you wrote and ask yourself if it is the truth. For example, if you wrote that you felt victimized by your partner having had an affair, is it true that they did anything to you? No. They simply took actions based on whatever they believed at the time. Ultimately, their choice had nothing to do with you. You are probably feeling victimized by the meaning you ascribe to your partner's affair in your mind.

2. Take the following actions for each item on your list:
   - Take responsibility for your inner guilt, shame, remorse, and projected anger.
   - Choose how to proceed forward in your life in a positive fashion (for example, pay back a debt, or apologize).
   - Forgive yourself and others involved for actions taken in non-awareness.

Love Note to Myself

I forgive myself for any harm generated by a lack of awareness of our shared divinity.

Forgive Your Body

Dear Body,

This is a long overdue letter… Since there is no time like the present, now is the perfect time for me to apologize to you for all the shit I have put you through for decades. I am sorry for not listening to you when I have had enough to eat and continued to stuff myself. I am sorry for not taking better care of you when I was tired and exhausted. I am sorry for letting you be used sexually when I didn't want to engage in sex. I am sorry for being judgmental and critical of how you looked and for thinking you didn't measure up. I am sorry for all the thoughts I have had about not being pretty enough, strong enough, sexy enough, or beautiful enough. Today is a new day. I vow to treat you with Love, compassion, kindness, appreciation, and respect. I ask for your forgiveness for all the ways I have mistreated and abused you in my thoughts, words, and actions. You are my home during this life, and I promise to make choices for your well-being—for the well-being of my body-mind-spirit. I commit to Lovingly care for you, because you are my perfect body. Thank you for being my body. You are beautiful. I am beautiful.

Love, Susyn

•

LESSON 4: FROM REJECTION TO GRATITUDE

It's also helpful to realize that this very body that we have, that's sitting right here right now—with its aches and its pleasures—is exactly what we need to be fully human, fully awake, fully alive.
—Pema Chodron

Most people I've known, particularly women, view their bodies through the lens of criticism, judgment, and disapproval. We aren't born with these judgments and criticisms—they are learned at a very early age.

In the process of growing up, we're socialized, domesticated, and programmed with concepts and ideas about what a perfect body is, including its size, shape, color, and weight. We then go on to spend much of our lives evaluating ourselves and others according to familial, cultural, and societal concepts of perfection that most often view women as objects rather than as living, breathing beings who deserve acceptance for who they are rather than being judged by their height, weight, breast size, age, skin tone, etc.

Dove's Campaign for Real Beauty cites the following global research, "Only 4 percent of women around the world consider themselves beautiful, and anxiety about appearance begins at an early age. Six out of ten girls are so concerned with the way they look that they opt out of participating fully in daily life—from going swimming and playing sports, to visiting the doctor, going to school, or even offering their opinions."

It is interesting to note that throughout human history, the notion of beauty has changed from one era to another and from one part of the world to another. The Three Graces painted by Peter Paul Rubens during the seventeenth century shows women who are round, shapely, and voluptuous, embodying a form that would be considered "fat" by the standards of today's runway models. In China, beginning in the seventh century and continuing for a thousand years, the practice of binding young girls' feet was commonplace, since small feet were an expression of beauty and social status. When I was a child in the 1950s, Clairol commercials seeded the idea in my redheaded mind that, "Blondes have more fun."

It is not necessary to determine which of these images is the true expression of beauty. Rather, be aware that your beliefs about physical beauty are concepts. If a belief is merely a made-up thought, the good news is that we can make up a new thought. When we judge, criticize, and belittle the way our bodies look, we experience disappointment, dissatisfaction, and shame.

This judging feeds our inner critic and separates us from gratitude and Love. This judging is a call for forgiveness.

Susyn's Story

I clearly remember the morning I became aware of the abusive thoughts I was directing toward my body with great conviction. I had just woken up. I was brushing my teeth when I caught a glimpse of myself in the bathroom mirror. Immediately, echoing through my mind, I heard the voice of judgment, loud and clear, 'I look disgusting. My hair's a mess. I'm just plain ugly. No wonder my husband wants a divorce. No one will ever love me again.'

For a few moments, I just stood looking at my reflection in the mirror, realizing how abusive and rejecting those thoughts were. I knew I had heard and spoken these thoughts hundreds, perhaps thousands of times throughout my life with absolute authority and conviction. That moment was a springboard for me. I realized that my critical thoughts were the glasses through which I viewed myself when I looked in a mirror. I had been unknowingly inflicting pain on myself through this form of self-inflicted domestic violence. I made a choice to honor, love, and express gratitude for my beautiful body—even on bad hair days when my shape doesn't align with an external standard of beauty, or when wrinkles appear—on all days.

PRACTICING THE LESSON

1. Notice the words you use that are critical and rejecting of your body. Here are some examples:
   - I hate my bald head.
   - My breasts are too small.
   - My cellulite is ugly.

- My body is too hairy.

- My penis is too small.

- My hair is too curly, frizzy, straight, or fine.

- I can't leave the house with this acne.

- I won't smile because my teeth are so crooked.

- I will never be beautiful with this prosthesis.

- I hate my fat thighs.

2. As soon as you notice your abusive programming, forgive yourself and make up a new thought honoring your body.

3. Write a letter to your body asking for forgiveness (see my letter on page 124-125). In her book *Self-Love: The Only Diet That Works*, Michelle Minero says, "Writing a body forgiveness letter is a powerful process because you're acknowledging the hurt you have caused your body and are asking for your body's forgiveness. By writing a body forgiveness letter, you're making peace with your body, admitting your self-criticisms and unhealthy care, and are committing to actively treat your body and yourself with Love."

LOVE NOTE TO MYSELF

My physical body is the perfect home for my divine spiritual essence.

•

LESSON 5: FROM DISEASE TO WELL-BEING

Underneath the illness, surgery, accidents, self-criticism, and blame exists a unique body-voice which delights in itself and is ever-seeking of more life. It calls for our embodiment. To forgive ourselves and our bodies means to reconnect with—and directly experience—our body-voice—whether through dialogue, drawing, journaling, storytelling, acting, movement, humor, ritual, or deep listening.
—Michelle James

Illness and disability are challenging. We assume that we're entitled to be well, and when we become sick, we often feel victimized and angry. Illness disrupts our schedules, it forces us to rest when we feel we don't have the time, and sometimes, it's simply painful. If we're born with or develop a physical or mental disability, we may be consumed by depression, anger, and hopelessness. We also have many theories about illness: some folks believe it's divine wrath, bad karma for sinful acts in previous lives, mentally created, genetically spawned, or just the normal course of life.

We've been given an amazing gift in life called "choice." During our lives, we experience whatever we need to learn, grow, and evolve. Perhaps we can view disease and illness as part of this experience. We're in the early stages of recognizing the power of the body-mind-spirit connection as the key to the entire expression of our reality, including the ability to heal—or to create illness. If you've never thought of taking ownership for your physical experience in this way, consider this point of view.

Recently, I watched the movie *Emmanuel's Gift*. The story focuses on a young man named Emmanuel Ofosu Yeboah who was born with a congenitally short leg. In the film, he not only transcends the beliefs of his own country, where such a disability is perceived as a family curse, but goes on to become an advocate for people with physical challenges. Rather than being a curse, his "disability" becomes a gift both for him and for the world.

Your attitude toward the human body—your body in particular—and illness is vital in generating your experience. Imagine for a moment that your physical body acts as a membrane between your Spiritual self and your ego-mind. When your mind is disturbed, your body responds in kind depending on the message it is receiving. If you spend your time thinking angry thoughts, for example, your body may respond with elevated blood pressure, digestive disorders, and headaches. By contrast, when you focus your attention on the people, places, things, and activities that are pleasurable, your body's response will likely be lowered blood pressure, a calm stomach, peace of mind, and relaxation.

When you are tuned-in to the sensations of your body, you may have a feeling of instant knowing when you are becoming ill. This is the way your intuition and the wisdom of spirit speaks through you. From this point of view, our body acts as an alarm system, alerting us when something is not quite right—it acts as an intermediary that assists us in negotiating between the spiritual and physical realms. Knowing this, being angry with our body for alerting us that something is wrong is like shooting the messenger for delivering unwanted news. We do not need to feel continually angry, resentful, or victimized by illness, and we do not have to make up stories to further upset or punish ourselves.

It is heart healing to acknowledge and allow yourself to feel whatever feelings are evoked by a medical diagnosis or by a physical, emotional, or spiritual challenge, but it is abusive and self-sabotaging to dwell on your anger, guilt, shame, fear, etc. Acknowledge and feel your feelings, and then focus on your well-being.

REMEMBER: Your mind commands your body to take action—or not to take action—based on your beliefs. If pain is too debilitating, seek the help, guidance, and expertise of a professional.

You may wonder if illness, disease, or a congenital condition is a bad thing or a good thing. These conditions are simply as they are, which is neither good nor bad—they are whatever meaning you ascribe to them. In the end, the quality of our lives and the emotional state of our being is a reflection of our chosen (conscious or unconscious) point of view—and that view may result in either dis-ease or a sense of well-being.

Donna Hadjipopov's Story

On October 29, 2015, my dear friend Donna Hadjipopov was diagnosed with cancer. Here is her story of the impact of her attitude on her healing:

"You have Stage 4 throat cancer," my brother solemnly said as I was recuperating from a surgical biopsy in New York's Mt. Sinai Medical Center.

Over the prior two years before the diagnosis, I had already lost everything of value in my life, including the sudden traumatic passing of my beloved husband due to cancer. After a moment of digesting this latest challenging news, I looked up to the heavens and simply said, "You have got to be kidding me!"

Two weeks later, seated across from the oncologists, I listened as they described the suggested protocol for my type of cancer, and I was horrified.

It entailed my needing a feeding tube because the radiation would scorch my throat, and my thyroid would be destroyed among other damages to my body, not to mention the additional side effects of chemotherapy. I questioned them about the possible secondary cancers caused by their treatment or the chance of this cancer returning, and they in turn were very nonchalant regarding my very real concerns.

After listening deeply to them, I questioned myself, "How could I possibly attack my throat in such a violent manner?!" When younger, I'd been a chef, and the taste of food was always an important factor in my daily joy of life. Furthermore, I have a sultry voice, and most importantly, my husband had fallen in love with it, and me, over the phone. I shared these two facts with the doctors and was met with more blank stares.

As someone who was raised to eat organic food and to take personal responsibility for my health, I couldn't comprehend filling my body with such powerful and toxic poisons. Though I needed time to reflect and to research my options, I was told not to take too long as they decreed me a painful death in six months to one year if I didn't follow their directives.

For some reason, I didn't see the expiration date that they saw stamped on my forehead.

My ultimate conclusion was that I could not harm my body in such a toxic manner, believing that my immune system if given a chance would heal me. I also faced the fact that I could very well die within the year, but if that were the case, it would be on my terms.

I got to work researching everything I could find about my particular diagnosis and cancer in general. I began to incorporate healing modalities each day that would honor all aspects of my being: body, mind, emotions, and spirit. Each morning while still in bed, I set the tone for my day with a healing meditation. In the evening, again in bed, a calming meditation *released any anxiety that I carried so I would be able to benefit from deep restorative sleep.*

I believe that the sense of balance and peace I derived from this ancient practice allowed me to be an active participant in my healing process as opposed to being in a constant state of fear, and anxiety. As I became spiritually strengthened, my resolve became stronger, and with it, my mind and intuition began to guide me.

Having a passion for living can seem daunting at times when confronted with enormous challenges such as the ones I'd had to face these past few years, but without the will to live, chances were slim that I would survive very long. I decided that I would go deeply into my very being to heal myself, no small task, as it meant looking at every aspect of my life.

As a direct result of this resolve, I deepened friendships, clarified others, and ended relationships that were not positive and filled with love. I confronted my failings, faults, and fears, which led me to forgive myself, which was even more daunting than forgiving others. With difficulty and practice, I learned how to ask for help—that was quickly responded to by my dear friends and family, reinforcing the power of community as an integral part of a healthy life. With deep gratitude, I began to give thanks every day for what I did have. And most telling, I began to love myself, truly love myself.

Then a miracle happened. I began to enjoy my life, to laugh, to dance, and to have fun. And to get better. I chose to live. My life has a richness and a joy in so many moments of each day as a direct result of my taking charge. I can say with conviction, I made the right choice.

June 2018 Update: Now, two and a half years later, after feasting on life, a recent scan indicated that not only has the cancer not spread, as predicted by all the 'specialists,' but the tumor is smaller!

As I reread Donna's story, two thoughts kept swirling around my mind; the first was the willingness and courage to forgive ourselves, and the second was the importance of choosing the healing path, which may or may not result in a cure, but which does, along with the power of forgiveness, heal our hearts and open our lives to the greatest gift of all, Love.

PRACTICING THE LESSON

1. To heal your heart of self-sabotaging beliefs, with a sense of curiosity, explore the beliefs you have about dis-ease and illness, including physical, mental, emotional, and spiritual challenges.

2. If you are ill now or have been in the past, reflect on the way you have chosen to perceive your experience. Answer the following questions:

   – Are you angry and resentful about your illness? Why? What are your beliefs?

   – Do you enjoy the attention you receive as a result of your condition? If yes, why? If no, why?

   – What purpose is your ailment serving?

   – What have you learned through this dis-ease?

   – How do you resist your ailments in your thoughts and actions?

   – Is your attitude one of war rather than acceptance?

   – Do you seek to blame your sickness on others? In what ways?

   – Do you consider your health challenges to be inconveniences that are interfering with the things you believe need to get done?

   – How can you take what you perceive as a curse and turn it into a gift?

3. Mary Baker Eddy started the Church of Christ, Scientist in 1879. She asserted that the mind could cause illness. Her assertions were challenging to the general thoughts of the public at the time. Charles

and Myrtle Fillmore founded Unity Church around 1889; they believed we are co-creators with God and that we create all our reality through thoughts held in mind. Dr. Ernest Holmes, who founded the International Religious Science movement in 1927, also believed in the healing of sickness through the power of the mind. What do you think about these ideas?

LOVE NOTE TO MYSELF

I forgive myself for not listening to the wisdom of my body, and I ask that she (my body) may speak loudl enough for me to hear and clearl enough for me to easily understand.

•

LESSON 6: FROM AGING TO EVOLVING

Many people can't stand the thought of aging, but it's the crystallized thought patterns and inflexible mind-sets that age people before their time. You can break through and challenge your crystallized patterns and mind-sets. That's what evolution and the expansion of love are about.
—Sara Paddison, *The Hidden Power of the Heart*

For many in the western world, aging is an enemy to be conquered. In recent years, the number of men and women having facelifts, Botox treatments, breast implants, liposuction, and a variety of other invasive and noninvasive procedures to capture the fountain of youth has exploded exponentially. At the same time, the vast numbers of dollars spent on anti-wrinkle creams and lotions continue to grow.

In our youth-obsessed culture, what happens when wrinkles appear, aches and pains greet us in the morning, or our sexual drive decreases? We look for a solution to recapture our youthful appearance and functioning, whether that means going under the knife or experimenting with lasers, injections, or magic blue pills. Inherent in this quest is the assumption that aging is bad, and that if I am the one who is aging, then I am losing my value and worth in the world.

Right now, acknowledge that aging is as natural as breathing. It's a made-up story to believe that one age is better than another, that younger is better than older. I wonder how many of us would truly want to repeat our teenage and young adult years, years when self-consciousness and self-loathing were often ruling our thoughts, especially when our ego-mind was busy judging, comparing, and evaluating every word we said and every action we took.

All life experiences reflect the cycle of germination, birth, growth, decline, and death. This process is neither good nor bad, neither right nor wrong; it is simply what is. Time spent denouncing what is fills our present moment with misery and unhappiness.

What would it take to appreciate and honor the process of our lives evolving? What would it take to forgive our bodies and minds for the natural process of aging? In indigenous cultures throughout the world, "elder" is an honored title. What if in our culture wrinkles were a symbol of a life fully lived and filled with the wisdom of experience?

A popular myth about aging is that our focus narrows, our beliefs become more rigid, and our bodies less flexible. We see examples of people all around us who defy this myth because they choose to live life to the fullest. Here's a story about my views on aging and how my mom, who died at age ninety-two, continues to inspire me to feast on the gift of life.

Susyn's Story

My parents were considered "old parents" by 1949 standards; my mother was thirty-nine and my father forty-eight when I was born. By the time I was eight, I was embarrassed that my parents were older than my friend's parents. I felt ashamed and assumed my friends thought less of me because my parents were "so old."

I'd wake up early on Sunday mornings, long before my parents and older sisters, and scrutinize the Sunday New York Times Magazine, staring at beautiful, young, sophisticated women and handsome, successful-looking suited men in the ads. Then I'd choose the couple I wished were my parents. Old and mature was bad, young and attractive was good.

It wasn't until I was in my late thirties (which seems quite young to me today, at sixty-nine!) that I began to appreciate having an older mom. I was inspired when at age seventy, after she'd lived in Manhattan most of her adult life and had been a widow for six years, she moved to another state and began a new chapter. I admired her at seventy-two when she joined a choir and sang in nursing homes each week. I was deeply moved when I videotaped her on her eighty-fifth birthday and she shared about her life, making sure that her lipstick was on before taping began. I shared in her delight as she described her ninetieth birthday celebration at her water aerobics class and how she and the fifty-three-year-old instructor had become close friends.

After years of shame and embarrassment about my "old" parents, I came to deeply appreciate what my mom had taught me about aging. Yes, it's true: she had aches and pains, doctor visits were part of her regular schedule, she became shorter, her skin turned wrinkly, her breasts hung low, and before her death at ninety-two, when I visited, it was a good idea to make sure a wheelchair was in the trunk of the car just in case she got too tired using her walker when we went out. But she taught me that age is, more than anything, simply a state of mind.

PRACTICING THE LESSON

1. Write your thoughts about the following questions:

   - Can you imagine forgiving your body and mind for the natural process of aging?

   - What is the impact on you of constant complaining and dissatisfaction with aging?

   - What if you upgraded the software of your mind to view aging as a gift, an opportunity to expand your capacity to give and receive Love and to generously share your gifts, talents, skills, and wisdom? How would this impact your daily life?

   - What if you truly embraced the wisdom that aging provides? What would change in your life?

   - What would be different for you, if as in indigenous cultures throughout the world, you believed that "elder" was an honored title and that your wrinkles were a symbol of a life fully lived?

2. Make a list of your judgments, criticisms, and complaints about aging. Then forgive yourself for believing those thoughts.

3. Write a story that demonstrates the gifts of aging and of a life forever evolving. Read your story aloud to at least one person. What did you learn by writing and reading your story?

4. Have a conversation with an elder and ask her/him to share the wisdom she/he has gleaned through her/his life. What was the impact of this conversation on you?

5. Create a ceremony to mark the passage from adult to elder.

LOVE NOTE TO MYSELF

I forgive myself for beliefs I have had up until now that dishonor the natural process of aging. I celebrate the gifts of being an elder.

Susyn's I am an Elder Ceremony

When I turned fifty years old, I began thinking about being an elder. I was readying myself to claim this honored title. I thought about and had many conversations about what being an elder meant to me on and off for the next fourteen years. I initially decided that I'd have a ceremony with the women who were most significant in my life as the centerpiece of my sixty-fifth birthday celebration. But two months before my birthday, I simply wasn't inspired by this idea.

I asked my dear friend Lorraine Simon, the founder of Moonfire Meeting House and The Women's Ways Mystery School, to create an I AM an Elder Ceremony with me. After our first conversation, I knew that what I wanted was a ceremony for me witnessed by Lorraine. We chose a date—ten days before my birthday. I sent an email to family and friends asking that they describe who I am in their lives, what they had learned through me, and their blessing for me as I stepped into the cherished role of Elder. Their responses warmed my heart. The evening before the ceremony, I wrote "My Intention for Being an Elder."

On the morning of the ceremony, I went for a walk on the beach. As I walked down the beach, I focused on all the gifts I had received in my life, including what I had learned from my challenging life experiences: deaths of family members, divorces, choosing to have an abortion to save a relationship that then ended three days after the abortion, miscarriages, and financial challenges. As I walked back up the beach, I read "My Intention for Being an Elder" aloud…allowing the words to be carried on the wind.

Returning to the house, I ceremoniously took a bath as though it was a baptism of sorts, submerging myself completely in the bathwater three times. As I dressed in clothes I love, time slowed down, allowing me to be mindful of every thought and action as I prepared for my sacred ceremony.

Lorraine arrived late in the afternoon. We created sacred space, smudged with sage, and laid out an altar with objects representing the four directions and the earth and sky. I called in my guides—family members who had long since crossed over, as well as teachers and friends who were my cheerleaders.

I went to the fireplace, where there was a roaring fire, read aloud "My Intention for Being an Elder," and then burned it. I read the beautiful notes my family and friends had sent to me and burned them; and finally, I passed some special pieces of jewelry through the fire to carry the energy of this day and the new elder chapter I was stepping into.

After an hour, I felt expansive and filled with Love, hope, and clarity about my 'marching orders' for my new role. Lorraine lovingly guided me to sit, close my eyes, and allow myself to be with this potent energy. I'm still not sure if I sat there for ten minutes or forty-five minutes. What I am sure of is that during the whole time, there were three words that kept repeating in my mind: "Standing Tall Woman." When I opened my eyes, the first words I said to Lorraine were, "I have been given a name for this chapter of my life."

I Am an Elder, I Am a Standing Tall Woman, and given the strife in the world today, I am committed to standing tall for life, liberty, and the pursuit of happiness and Love for All.

Forgive Your Family

If there is anything that we wish to change in the child,
we should first examine it and see whether it is not
something that could better be changed in ourselves.
—C.G. Jung, Integration of the Personality, 1939

•

LESSON 7: FROM DISAPPOINTMENT TO HONORING

It's natural for parents to desire the best for their children. When gazing at their newborn, parents have glimpses of an imagined future. In this future, their child is healthy, loved, satisfied with their work, and has the financial abundance to enjoy a full life. While these are admirable wishes, too often parents have fixed ideas of how their children's lives should look and the road their children should follow. Parents' expectations may arise because of a road not taken in their own lives, the desire to uphold a family tradition, or wanting an easier path for the child they Love.

Expectations for our children often lead to disappointment. For example, your child gets in trouble in school (and you're disappointed with her poor behavior), or your son doesn't try out for the football team and wants to take dance lessons (and you're disappointed because everyone knows that dance is for sissies and football is for young men). Perhaps your daughter's first serious romantic relationship is with someone of another race, or the same gender (and you're disappointed and worried that she's not considering the future problems that may arise from this choice). Late in the night, you receive a call from the police that your child has been arrested for selling drugs (disappointment, anger, and heartbreak).

As much as parents may think that their children "belong to them," they are on their own journey in life. We can Love our children and illuminate a path for them, but when we're disappointed in them, our disappointment is a reflection of the incongruence between our beliefs of how their life should be and the way their lives are unfolding.

"On Children"
Kahlil Gibran, from *The Prophet*, 1923

Your children are not your children.
They are the sons and daughters of Life's longing for itself.
They come through you but not from you,
And though they are with you, yet they belong not to you.

You may give them your love but not your thoughts.
For they have their thoughts.
You may house their bodies but not their souls,
For their souls dwell in the house of tomorrow,
which you cannot visit, not even in your dreams.
You may strive to be like them but seek not to make them like you.
For life goes not backward nor tarries with yesterday.
You are the bows from which your children as living arrows are sent forth.
The archer sees the mark upon the path of the infinite,
and He bends you with His might that His arrows may go swift and far.
Let your bending in the archer's hand be for gladness;
For even as He loves the arrow that flies,
so He loves also the bow that is stable.

Gibran's poem, published almost one hundred years ago, is a call to honor our children as life's continuous desire to express itself. We can Love our children and guide them, however, when we are disappointed in them and place conditions on our love, conflict and dissatisfaction are bound to occur.

Susyn's Story

I clearly remember the night in 1974 when I called my mother and told her that my then-husband and I were buying a camper and planning to travel cross-country for a year. I heard her gasp and then scream at me, "What's wrong with you? You have a beautiful house, a great job, and you're married. Why are you doing this to me?"

Of course, my mom was judging my choices by her standards and her ideas of how a happy life should look for her twenty-five-year-old daughter. I was not meeting her expectations. Naturally, she wanted what was best for me, but her beliefs about "the good life" blinded her from realizing that I was sharing my heart song with her.

Isn't it time to forgive your children for not doing what you wanted them to do? Isn't it time to free yourself from the expectations that are causing conflict and dissension between you and your children? In your heart of hearts, of course, you only want the best for them, so why criticize and judge their choices harshly? Isn't it time to honor their experience with unconditional love, share your wisdom without judgments, and guide them to listen to the wisdom of their hearts?

PRACTICING THE LESSON

1. Sit quietly with a photo of your child. As you look at the photo, make a list of all ways that she/he has seemingly disappointed and hurt you. Forgive yourself for taking your child's actions personally. When you have completed this, either in writing or verbally, tell

your child that you Love and honor her/him unconditionally. What did you learn through this exercise?

2. Write down the expectations you have for your child—each should, ought-to, and I-know-what-is-best-for-you. When your list is complete, as a symbol of forgiving and freeing yourself of past disappointments and emotional wounds based on your unmet expectations, burn the list and use the ashes to fertilize a plant. How do you feel having completed this powerful ritual?

3. Have a conversation with your child and tell her/him what you honor and celebrate about his/her presence in your life. Share the lessons you have learned about yourself through your sacred relationship with your child. How has this conversation influenced your thinking about your children?

LOVE NOTE TO MYSELF

> *I forgive myself for the expectations and rules I place upon my children. I forgive my children for not fulfilling my expectations. I honor my children as full expressions of the divine and for the opportunities they offer me to embody and express unconditional Love.*

•

LESSON 8: FROM CONTROL TO PARENTING

All the time a person is a child, he is both a child and learning to be a parent. After he becomes a parent, he becomes predominantly a parent reliving childhood.
—Benjamin Spock, MD

Is there a more challenging and rewarding endeavor than raising children as far as our spiritual development is concerned? Children test every aspect of our belief system. They're the first to point out when we're not walking our talk. One of the best ways to lose the respect of a child is to say, "Do as I say, not as I do."

When we were children, we made many judgments about the way our parents should be, how much love we were receiving, and if that love was expressed in the way we desired. As children, we judged everything about our parents. These assessments were made from a child's point of view, one that did not comprehend the whole story or circumstances of what was going on at the time.

Those memories, judgments, and assessments remain in our minds as adults, and we either follow through in raising our children as our parents raised us, or we do the opposite in reaction to our childhood experiences (or a combination of both). This observation is what Dr. Spock is alluding to in the quote at the beginning of this lesson.

The key to being the best parent possible is to avoid the trap of reactive parenting. To do this, we must look deeply within ourselves and at what we believe about our childhood, our parents, and what it means to be a parent through the eyes of compassion.

When, as parents, we take our old childhood wants, wounds, and needs and impose them onto our children's lives—this is reactive parenting. We avoid this trap by being awake to our children's' needs in the present moment rather than making choices based on how our parents raised us. Let's say you were raised by a strict disciplinarian who punished first and asked questions later. Now, you are not sure if you should treat your children the same way or if you should swear off discipline altogether, since your childhood was marred by constant punishment. The answer to this dilemma is quite simple; give a child who is responsible some leeway, and provide discipline for a child who needs clear boundaries and limits for their well-being and safety. Make your decisions based on your child's individual needs, not on your automatic, reactive, habitual response.

There is a fine balance between creating a flexible structure for children to grow up safely versus creating a limiting and stifling prison. Every parent, in their heart of hearts, wants their children to be safe, prosperous, and happy. But when parents exert continuous control over their children's every thought and action, they are unknowingly setting themselves up for a lifetime of resentment and struggle with their children.

Vivian Glyck, author of *The Tao of Poop: Keeping Your Sanity and Your Soul While Raising a Baby* shared her personal experience:

> *"We cannot interfere with the natural processes that our children must go through in life. So often, what seems harsh or cruel as we're experiencing it with our children is in reality strengthening them for the time ahead.*
>
> *"I'm often reminded of the story of the little boy who sees a butterfly beating its wings wildly as it tries to emerge from its cocoon. The butterfly appears as though it will die in its furious attempt to break free. Desperate to help, the little boy pulls the cocoon apart and frees the butterfly. Although the butterfly springs out, it immediately falls to the ground and dies.*
>
> *"The only way a butterfly can strengthen its wings is by beating them against the walls of the cocoon. In his attempts to help, the boy prevented the butterfly from developing the strength it would need to survive. Likewise, our job as parents is not to keep our children free from all suffering. Forgive yourself and keep letting go each time you find yourself gripping tighter. Trust that your children will learn on their own."*

Every person must transcend their childhood and forgive their parents' mistakes to be happy. In turn, children ideally will eventually learn to forgive parents for their decisions made out of fear and the belief that they always know what is best for their children. The difficult part is forgiving ourselves because we feel so guilty for hurting our children and for imposing our will on them.

> **REMEMBER:** Guilt is a strategy of the ego-mind to exert control. We cannot change what we have done in the past, but we can reframe—transform—our point of view about the past.

Let go of the guilt and shame. Know that you did the best job you could've done at that time based on the awareness you had then. We can forgive ourselves for the choices we made in the past and make new choices in the present moment based on our ever-evolving awareness of Heart Healing.

PRACTICING THE LESSON

1. Make a list of all the mistakes for which you feel guilt and shame as a parent.
   - Look at each item and ask yourself if you would take the same action again if you were functioning at the same level of awareness again. (Of course, you would.) Do not use your current level of awareness to judge what you did back then.
   - Next to each item on your list, write the declaration: I forgive myself for _____.
   - When you are finished, burn the list and cut the strings of attachment to your guilt and shame.
   - What did you learn by doing this exercise?
2. List the beliefs about parenting that support the awareness you have today.

3. Have a conversation with your children about your new awareness about parenting.

LOVE NOTE TO MYSELF

> *I forgive myself for any of my words and actions that resulted in pain and suffering for the children in my life. I acknowledge that I was doing the best I could based on my understanding at the time. I express my unconditional Love for my children today.*

•

LESSON 9: FROM RESENTMENT TO UNCONDITIONAL LOVE

I've learned that regardless of your relationship with your parents, you'll miss them when they're gone from your life.
—Maya Angelou

Parents generally receive the brunt of the blame for their children's unhappiness and misery in life. Countless therapy sessions are devoted to moving through anger, blame, and animosity directed toward parents. Either they smothered us with their love, abused us with their words and actions, or failed to provide the guidance and Love we thought we should have had.

A client recently told me that she'd been thinking about her father. He had died ten years ago. She said, "During the past few days, I've begun to feel compassion when I think of my dad." I don't think her story is unusual.

I spent much of my life, starting as a pre-teen, being annoyed and resenting my parents. Simply that they lived and breathed was annoying to me because they didn't do things, say things, or act the way I thought they should. (Of course, I knew I was right—so many of my girlfriends were acting the same way toward their parents! We were a Misery Loves Company Support Group constantly complaining about our parents.)

But what if our parents are the perfect parents for us? Rather than resenting them, we can imagine that even the most painful actions on their part have assisted us in becoming the people we are today. Isn't it time to forgive, let go of old resentments, and see our parents through the eyes of unconditional Love?

REMEMBER: You may or may not get the response you desire when you forgive. The purpose of forgiving is to heal your heart by letting go of the emotional wounds of the past.

In 2009, when I lived in Arizona, I had the honor of getting to know Brenda Adelman; and I have been inspired by her powerful forgiveness story. Since then, with a degree in spiritual psychology, Brenda has written *My Brooklyn Hamlet*, a one-woman show based on her life story which she has performed all around the world. Her work today focuses on helping people transform pain into healing narratives. Here's Brenda's story:

> *I had a very close relationship with my parents; perhaps too close, as I fulfilled the emotional needs they couldn't fulfill for one another. In 1995, I moved away from New York to live with my fiancé in California, and during that first year, my parents visited several times. On their last trip, they seemed to be getting on a lot better. So, I was surprised when my mom*

called to tell me they were separating. She sounded okay, although she told me my father had been cheating on her.

A few days later, as I returned from a weekend workshop, my fiancé broke the terrible news. He said there'd been an accident with a gun and my darling mother was dead.

It was eight hours before the body was discovered, by which time my father had a lawyer in place, there had been a cleanup in the house, and no gun was found at the scene of the crime. I immediately flew to New York and went with my half-brother to see my father, who explained they'd been fighting and one of them had pulled the trigger.

Within days, my father had contacted my mother's older sister, who ended up being there for him in a very peculiar way. He moved in with her, and sometime later, they got married.

In the meantime, my father had been charged with second-degree murder, but because the weapon, his gun, was never recovered, his sentence was reduced to five years in prison for involuntary manslaughter. He got out in two and a half years for good behavior.

At first, unable to bear the thought of losing both my parents, I wouldn't accept that my father had meant to kill my mother. My brother disagreed, and because he felt the system hadn't held my father/his step-father accountable (two and a half years for what he believed was cold-blooded murder), he decided to pursue the only other avenue he had, which was a civil lawsuit. I disagreed, and as a result, my brother and I stopped speaking to each other for six years.

After my mom's death, I felt a deep sense of shame and despair. What did it say about me if this is what had happened to my parents?

The only thing that helped transform these negative emotions was writing my story. I was enrolled in an acting course in LA at the time, so I wrote and performed a fifteen-minute personal piece, at the end of which

I noticed people crying. I was amazed because instead of being judged for what I'd revealed, I received a standing ovation and so much empathy and compassion.

While my Dad was in prison, I wrote to him several times asking him to tell me what had happened. He ignored my questions, and in the end, we stopped communicating. Later, when he was out of prison, he contacted me again. I was pleased to hear from him until I realized he was only interested in getting his hands on my inheritance money. He was toxic, and I decided to pursue the civil court case with my brother. I was still desperate for my father to tell the truth and assumed he would have to take the stand.

I thought he would show up at court, but he never did. He skipped town and went to Florida, transferring his money into offshore accounts. My aunt also disappeared. Although we won the case—we won a judgment of 2.2 million dollars for the wrongful death of our mom—my brother and I never collected a cent, and I ended up paying tens of thousands of dollars in fees to my lawyer.

To help me deal with the pain during all this time, I was trying to forgive. But I didn't know how, as I assumed forgiveness was about reconciliation, and I didn't want my dad back in my life. However, during the process, I realized forgiveness also meant resolving inner conflict and clearing my heart of hate; it meant that if I thought about my father, my day wasn't wrecked anymore.

The missing step was embracing my anger in a healthy way. I still felt a deep level of anger at myself for ever having trusted my father, which was demonstrated by my overeating. I had so much self-judgment. You can't forgive someone else unless you've forgiven yourself. It was while taking a course in spiritual psychology that I recognized how with each negative thought directed at my father, I was re-wounding myself.

Suddenly, I had an insight into the oneness of 'us.' I was inwardly guided to go to the top of a mountain in Los Angeles and carry out a ceremony of release using one of my father's hats, which I threw over the mountain side. With this simple ritualistic gesture, something was released inside of me. From that moment, I wasn't burdened anymore.

As for forgiving my aunt, that has been much more difficult, but I strive to be able to let go of any righteousness I may feel about her because I know that this little bit of righteousness will only continue to hurt me.

In 2004, I received a letter in the mail from my aunt's attorney with a copy of my father's death certificate saying he'd died of a heart attack. It was a relief in a way, because I realized there had been a part of me trying to get my dad back; but now reconciliation was no longer possible. At that point, something settled in me, and for the first time since my mother's death, I was able to properly grieve.

PRACTICING THE LESSON

1. Write a letter to each of your parents, whether or not they are alive or are active in your life. Tell them what you appreciate about them. Send the letter (if it comes from Love), have a conversation with them about it, or visualize a conversation with them. Notice what you are feeling and thinking as you do this exercise.

2. Write a new story of your life in which you describe why your parents are the perfect parents for you.

LOVE NOTE TO MYSELF

I forgive my parents unconditionally. I see them as expressions of the divine. I realize they did the best they could.

•

LESSON 10: FROM RIVALRY TO RESPECT

Notice how much harder you are on your siblings than [on] total strangers. If you were meeting someone for the first time and they were ten minutes late, they'd say, "I'm sorry," and you'd likely say, "No problem." If your sibling was late, you might remember all the times he or she was late. You might attribute unflattering motives to their tardiness. Instead, give your siblings the same respect that you would anyone else.
—Richard Carlson

Many of us are familiar with the Old Testament story of the rivalry between two brothers, Cain and Abel. Cain, the older of the two, was constantly expected to help care for his younger brother, Abel. Over time, Cain became annoyed and frustrated with Abel. Cain resented the expectations and responsibilities he had as an older brother. Finally, Cain's anger towards Abel grew, and he murdered Abel.

The concept of sibling rivalry has been part of our collective consciousness for as long as we can remember. I often wonder if the warring in the world today is an exaggerated expression of sibling rivalry. If we truly are one, then we each are one another's brothers and sisters—we're siblings. Since sibling relationships can be very challenging, if we have difficulty seeing the divine in our blood siblings—then it's easy to understand the fighting, blaming, bullying, terrorizing, and murder that continues to be repeated in the world.

It is normal human development to seek out mirrors to help define ourselves as individuals. Without the reflections provided by our siblings and parents, it is hard to know who we are and what our position is in our family structure. There are so many unwritten family rules siblings help us learn. We learn how to assert ourselves through our experiences with them, or not. We use them to perfect and hone the personalities that we then present to the larger world.

If you are the younger child, you may start out admiring and doing your best to emulate your older siblings, endowing them at times with superhuman qualities. So it is confusing when your hero directs their animosity toward you for no apparent reason. Then there is the form of sibling rivalry that occurs due to gender differences. "Daddy's Girl" may be the apple of dad's eye, and no matter what you do as a son, you may then never perceive your father's love for you as equal to the love he bestows upon your sister.

The mere existence of an additional child or children in the family could signify Less. Less time alone with parents. Less attention for hurts and disappointments. Less approval for accomplishments... No wonder children struggle so fiercely to be first or best. No wonder they mobilize all their energy to have more or most. Or better still, all.
—Adele Faber

This rivalry is then magnified as children vie for the attention of their parents. The child who receives their parent's attention is the winner, and the other is the loser. The ego-mind develops by defining itself as different and separate from others, and it is important that our parents validate our existence with their attention. If we believe that our parents are paying more attention to our siblings, subconscious wounds may play themselves out over a lifetime of interactions.

These dynamics set up daily habits of thought and behavior in which judging, comparing, and keeping score become the norm. Often, in their unawareness, parents will pit one child against the other as a means to inspire them to do better. In the end, they may create resentment and frustration among their children. From the time we were children, we were unconsciously programmed to be rivals rather than to respect and appreciate our difference. How do we free ourselves from the frustrations of sibling rivalry that began long before that concept was in our vocabulary?

Here's a snippet of a conversation I had about sibling relationships with Dr. Frederic Luskin, author of *Forgive for Good: A Proven Prescription for Health and Happiness*:

"What if someone offered you $20,000,000 (that's right, twenty million dollars,) to let go of all of your anger toward your siblings? Of course, you could do it—right? Well, if that's true, it means that the only thing that is keeping you from forgiveness is your motivation. You grew up with these people and you love them, so why not motivate yourself to forgive? It's easier than you think."

We may never know for sure why our siblings are our siblings, whether it was by divine design or random chance. What we do know is that the human you call brother or sister, stepbrother or stepsister, or half-sister or half-brother is an expression of the divine. Are you learning about unconditional Love from your sibling, or is the rivalry expanding and deepening as the years go on?

Are you a victim in this relationship, a persecutor, or do you dance between the two? Isn't it time to forgive for your peace of mind, and to honor, respect, and see the perfection of your siblings?

PRACTICING THE LESSON

1. Identify a situation that is a source of discord between you and your sibling(s).

   – Make a list of the beliefs you have about your sibling(s), yourself, and your relationship(s) that is fueling the discord.

   – What prevents you from letting go of anger, resentment, and hostility toward your sibling(s)?

   – Even if you believe they have done you wrong, apologize for any way you may have hurt them.

   – Forgive them for past rivalries.

   – Make a list of the contributions they have made to your life and let them know how much you appreciate and Love them.

   – What did you learn through this exercise?

LOVE NOTE TO MYSELF

I forgive my siblings. I ask for forgiveness from my siblings. Sibling relationships—and 80 percent of Americans have at least one—outlast marriages, survive the death of parents, resurface after quarrels that would sink any friendship. They flourish in a thousand incarnations of closeness and distance, warmth, loyalty, and distrust.

—Erica E. Goode

•

LESSON 11: FROM FEUDING TO HARMONY

You don't choose your family. They are God's gift to you,
as you are to them.
—Desmond Tutu

At my "Opening the Door to Heart Healing" workshops, I often ask, "How many of you are aware of a feud in your family where one person or family group refuses to speak to another?" It always amazes me to find between 50–75% of the audience raising their hands!

What does this say about the human state of affairs regarding forgiveness? Yep, we're not very good at it. When feuds and resentments in families live on and on, often through multiple generations, it isn't surprising to see the same dynamics in our workplace, community, city, state, country, and the world. Do you desire to live in a more peaceful and Loving world? Then you must heal the wounds at home.

We often assume that because we are related, our points of view and the way we see life should be similar. However, familial genetics do not assure agreement when it comes to beliefs, opinions, and judgments!

As far as our friends go, we generally choose people whose belief systems align with ours. We purposely pick friends because they continually reinforce our viewpoint. When it comes to family, we don't choose them according to whether or not their point of view agrees with ours—we get what we get, as Desmond Tutu states in the quote at the beginning of this lesson.

How do we deal with feisty relatives and family situations? We start with understanding that everyone is entitled to their point of view, whether we agree with their perspective or not. If both parties cannot detach from their perspective or at least learn to allow another point of view, then the only thing we can do is agree to disagree. However, seeing things from another's perspective creates an opening for understanding, compassion, discussion, and unconditional Love. Aren't the qualities of love and harmony the foundation we desire in our family?

Make the time to forgive yourself for any family discord that you either participated in or perpetuated. As an expression of your commitment to healing your heart, forgive your family for any actions they took against you in their need to be right, even it if meant they were stubborn and contentious. If your family members are not interested in forgiving, that's okay—you've done your part to heal and open your heart. Who knows what might happen in the future as a result of your action? Miracles are always possible.

PRACTICING THE LESSON

1. If you have decided to not speak to a family member, consider forgiving them for whatever you believe they did or did not do. Write a letter:

   – Asking for their forgiveness for imposing your point of view on them.

   – Acknowledge their point of view (whether or not you agree with it) and that you would rather they be a part of your family than hold resentment in your heart towards them.

   – Do not defend your point of view anywhere in the letter—that is not forgiveness! It is up to you whether or not you send that letter. Remember it takes courage to detach from the desire to be right. I encourage you to go beyond what you believe you are capable of. Go ahead—create a miracle.

   – Write your reflections on this exercise.

2. If a family member is not speaking to you because of actions you took that they did not agree with:

– Review the situation to make sure you were not rigid and self-righteous.

– If you were, ask for their forgiveness, making sure not to defend your point of view.

– If this is not your situation, then send them a note letting them know you wish to move beyond the discord in the family. Ask, "What can I do to help reconcile the situation?" Light a seven-day candle and pray for harmony in your family.

– If they do answer with a suggestion, it is up to you to decide whether or not you can follow through with their suggestion. Ask yourself, "What would Love do here?" when deciding how to respond to their suggestion(s).

– If you do not get a response, say a prayer for the highest good of all, and let it go.

– Write your reflections on this exercise.

Love Note to Myself

I open my heart and mind to the divine alive in all of my family members—including me!

Forgive Your Relationships

My friend, Sheri Rosenthal, founder of Wanderlust Entrepreneur, recalls:

"When I first started on my spiritual path, my teacher gave me a powerful personal assignment. He asked me to thank my ex-husband for having an

affair, meeting his new wife, and divorcing me. I found his request a bit shocking, and so did my ex-husband! He was taken aback when I thanked him for having the affair and asked me why I would share this with him. I explained that I no longer desired to be a victim of any situation. Living my life from gratitude was my goal.

"Originally, I could only see the affair as a bad thing—but later I realized it could be seen as bad or good, depending on whether I wanted to be a victim or a victorious co-creator of my life. When I finally took responsibility for my life, I realized I had co-created the affair with him (it always takes two to tango). I was able to have gratitude for the experience and forgive both of us for our non-awareness."

●

LESSON 12: FROM OPPOSITION TO SACRED UNION

I first learned the concepts of non-violence in my marriage.
—Mohandas K. Gandhi

The dynamics of marriage and partnership are a microcosmic reflection of national and global politics. There's conflict, war, reconciliation, and harmony—all present in one bedroom! Conflict and opposition arise when we are more attached to defending our beliefs as the right and therefore only possible point of view, than to Loving one another. The problem is that there are too many viewpoints in the bedroom, including:

- "What is"—the actual physical, emotional, mental, and spiritual aspects of each person.
- Who I think my partner is.

- Who my partner thinks I am.

- Who I think my partner thinks I am.

- Ideas my partner and I have about ourselves, including, "I'm not good enough," "The people I love abandoned me," "I don't trust men," "I don't trust women," "I'm shy," "I have a great sense of humor," "I'm handsome," "I'm loving," etc.

- Personal beliefs of each partner regarding relationships, marriage, and everything else in life.

That is one busy bedroom! When we project our ideas about marriage, relationships, running a home, having children, and hundreds of other issues onto our partners—and they do the same to us—we create a wall between us that can make it difficult to get to the other side. We get more involved in defending our beliefs than Loving one another, and the result is often conflict and opposition.

I know very few people who haven't had the opportunity—just when we think we have had enough of these opportunities!—to grow and learn about themselves within the context of a Love partnership and union. A partner is a mirror reflecting our expression of divine unconditional Love, as well as at times reflecting to us our expression of the Wicked Witch of the West or the Hulk!

Forgiveness allows us to evolve our old points of view and ways of perceiving the world, opening us up to amazing experiences. Rewrite those old victim stories taking responsibility for your creation. A Loving relationship is the playground for emotional and spiritual growth.

PRACTICING THE LESSON

1. Below is a list of items for which to forgive yourself and your partner. Personalize the list so it applies to you and is complete.

Sit with each item until you can truly forgive it and let go. If you get stuck, light a candle for that item and pray for clarity, an open heart, and the wisdom of spirit. If forgiveness does not come immediately, return to that item until you have let it go completely. Trust that the timing is perfect. Some issues are forgiven quickly, others take longer; that's simply, "what is." I forgive my partner, ex-partner, and myself for:

- Having an affair
- Physical or emotional abuse
- Gossiping to others about our relationship
- Taking sides against one another
- Having expectations about how love should be expressed
- Disregarding one another's needs and desires
- Being emotionally unavailable
- Judging our physical bodies
- Being sexually unavailable
- Being unsupportive of one another
- Insulting one another in front of other people
- Using our children against one another
- Being continually angry, depressed, or hypercritical
- Feeling victimized
- Allowing oneself to be treated badly
- Not respecting each other
- Not Loving oneself 100 percent
- Believing you must settle in life
- Not feeling worthy enough to deserve a great partner
- Being unaware of what we were creating in the relationship
- Blaming our unhappiness on one another

- Staying in an unhealthy relationship out of fear

- Failing to recognize the gift(s) in the relationship

- Judging one another

- Choosing a partner who you knew was trouble from the start

- Wanting to change one another—not accepting him or her as is

- Only giving conditional love

- Being rude and unkind

- Closing your heart to one another

2. Rewrite your Love story. This is a powerful opportunity for self-discovery and Heart Healing.

LOVE NOTE TO MYSELF

Love relationships shine the light on whatever I do not Love about myself and on the beliefs, conscious or unconscious, I have about Love. Love relationships are an opportunity to heal wounds of the past. My relationship with myself is the blueprint for all my Love relationships.

•

LESSON 13: FROM EXPECTATIONS TO UNDERSTANDING

People do what they are going to do, and it isn't always what we want, wish, or hope for.
—Sheri Rosenthal

It can be said that expectations are the root of all evil. Think about it; if you didn't have expectations of people and situations, you would never have cause to be upset about anything! We expect our friends are going to show up on time for a lunch date, that the business contract we signed will come to fruition, and that no one will cut us off in traffic. We can have all the expectations we want of people, but it doesn't mean we are going to get what we want from them—even if they promised—or we may get what we expected, but not the way we expected.

Every person is doing the best they can from their current point of view and level of consciousness. Measuring others against our yardsticks is not productive. Other people may or may not have all the same beliefs as you. When you impose your beliefs on others, the result is often pain and suffering for everyone.

Whenever I talk about these ideas, people say that expectations are necessary or no one will do anything. However, think about this for a minute. When we say that, we are making the assumption that without a contractual arrangement—whether it is verbal or written—people will not be inspired to follow through on their word. If we need the threat of retribution to force people to do what they have promised, this means that humanity is not a very responsible bunch. However, when we are impeccable with our word—honest, speaking our truth—we will do our best to follow through with what we have said to cultivate trust in our relationships.

We live most successfully when we all operate from wanting to do our best because we enjoy doing so and it makes our heart sing—as opposed to being under the whip of a feisty belief system filled with expectations telling us we must perform in a certain way to be good enough and worthy. In one case, we are living as the reflection of the Loving Energy of the Universe moving through us; in the other, we are living the will of our domesticated ego-mind. One way of living is fulfilling and limitless, and the other is limiting, controlling, and rigid.

It is helpful to understand why people do not follow through with what they have promised so that one is able to have compassion for them, rather than feeling anger and frustration and taking their words and actions personally. Below is a list you can use for greater clarity about the words and deeds of others, as well as your own!

- Sometimes, we simply forget what we have promised.

- Sometimes, we believe we have followed through with what was promised and the other person was expecting something more or different.

- Sometimes, we have every intention of doing what we promised, but our unconscious beliefs of "I am not good enough" cause us to sabotage ourselves.

- Sometimes, people simply do not tell the truth.

- Sometimes, people have difficulty saying, "No."

Whatever the situation, the bottom line is this: It's not about us. People do what they are going to do, and it isn't always what we wish, hope for, or want. When we remember this statement, our lives are happier. Let's forgive others for their side of the situation and forgive ourselves for imposing our belief systems and our expectations on others and for using their actions (or lack thereof) to upset ourselves.

"I have learned that as long as I hold fast to my beliefs and values—and follow my moral compass—then the only expectations I need to live up to are my own."
—Michelle Obama

PRACTICING THE LESSON

1. Take a few moments to identify five times you have imposed your expectations on others and been disappointed. Consider your family, your employees, your partner, politicians, and even yourself.

   – Understanding the myriad reasons why people behave the way they do, are you willing to open your heart to compassion and understanding for what has occurred? If not, why not?

   – Does understanding that at every moment each of us is taking actions based on our personal beliefs help you to detach from your angry reaction? If not, why? What would it take for you to change your point of view?

   – Forgive yourself and the other person(s) in each of your five situations by taking action—either by saying so verbally, writing them a note, sending flowers, or through a creative act of your choosing.

   – What are the lessons of this exercise for you?

LOVE NOTE TO MYSELF

I forgive myself for imposing my expectations and beliefs on others and for allowing myself to be upset when others fail to meet my expectations.

•

LESSON 14: FROM NON-AWARENESS TO GRACE

Each of us at any time and space is doing the very best
we can with what we have.
—Louise L. Hay

Our thoughts and actions are a direct reflection of our consciousness and current level of awareness. Using a computer analogy, our awareness is based on the software installed. Our parents, cultural and societal morals, the media, and those people and organizations we perceive as authorities have programmed our software. This domestication is based on thoughts voiced with authority and conviction that, consciously or unconsciously, we have agreed are the truth. Once the programming is installed, it functions as an invisible filter directly influencing every relationship and experience we have.

Each version of the software has rules and beliefs about the behaviors and actions of ourselves and others. When the beliefs and behaviors of others are congruent with ours, then peaceful coexistence and a magnificent harmony are possible. If the ideas and behaviors of others are at odds with our beliefs, however, there is conflict, anger, and blame.

Given that each of us perceives the world through our programming at every moment, our actions are always aligned with what we think. If you want to know what you believe, take a look at what is going on in your life. This means that every action, whether or not we agree with it, is the very best that a person can do based on their level of awareness at that moment. When you take the time to listen to the reasons someone had for joining a gang, committing acts of violence, having an affair, or failing to remember your birthday, you will discover that their behavior is understandable based on how they perceive the world at that moment. I am not suggesting that you condone violent, hateful, abusive behavior; rather, I say this so you will deeply understand—grok—the power of your beliefs in creating your experience.

Are we completely at the mercy of this programming and doomed to these habitual patterns of thinking? No, not at all. At every moment, we can shift our awareness and upgrade the software of our mind. The most life-affirming upgrade is the one that states, "I am a mighty expression of Love in the world." When faced with conflict, this program does not hold fast to a position of right or wrong or good or bad. Instead, it poses the question, "What would Love do here?" Then your task is to listen o and follow the wisdom of your open heart.

Our programming can also lead to the habit of taking things personally, which most often is a direct path to suffering. Consider this example; your spouse cancels plans for your birthday at the last minute because of an unexpected problem at work. You feel hurt, unloved, and angry as he explains that he will make it up to you. What you are thinking is, 'If he loved me, he would not always be putting work first, especially on my birthday.' You meet your friends for your birthday dinner, and as each one asks where your husband is, you can feel your fury growing. Your birthday is ruined.

Even though you were celebrating with your closest friends, your attention is hooked by the thought that your husband always winds up disappointing you. By taking his actions personally and feeling as though they were daggers piercing your heart, you end up suffering and blaming it on him.

One dimension of forgiveness would be to forgive him for not being at your birthday dinner and making an alternate plan to celebrate your special day. An act of grace and even deeper expression of forgiveness would be to forgive yourself for using someone else's actions to cause yourself suffering and misery.

Susyn's Story

I remember how unworthy of ever being loved I felt in the midst of my divorce. Two days after I moved out of our house, his girlfriend moved in. This incident was a perfect reflection of my programming: 'You'll never be happy in love. You ruin all your relationships with men. All men wind up leaving you.' In the days that followed, I decided to change this script, since all it did was result in suffering and unhappiness in my life.

I focused my attention on a simple mantra: I am Loved. I installed this software in my conscious awareness: I wrote it as an affirmation. When I saw my reflection in a mirror, I said it in addition to repeating it aloud whenever it popped into my mind. I randomly wrote it on pages of my calendar. Whenever I began to indulge in a pity party, I would say, "Oops" and repeat the mantra—sometimes more times than I could count during a particular day. While our marriage did not turn out the way I imagined, the relationship ultimately expanded my awareness and deepened my capacity to be, give, and receive Love. In fact, I have since thanked my ex-husband for what I learned about being loving through our relationship.

* * *

The bottom line is, most people believe they're making conscious life choices when in fact they are responding to the software of their mind. This is not true awareness; it is not mindfulness. Our actions express grace when we make our choices based on the wisdom of our hearts rather than the knowledge lodged in our programming. Every moment, we can have a new thought and create new brain pathways to upgrade the software of our mind. Being forgiving and letting go are the keys to this software upgrade.

PRACTICING THE LESSON

1. Identify a relationship in your life that causes you pain and suffering.

   – What do you believe about this relationship?

   – How are your beliefs perpetuating your pain and suffering?

   – With your newfound awareness, identify the gifts you have been graced with through this relationship.

   – Forgive yourself for your non-awareness.

   – Thank the other person involved for offering you the opportunity to free yourself from self-destructive programming.

2. Think about all the male-female relationships you have had in your life. As an exercise in expanding your awareness, forgive all men for the way they have treated you as a woman, or forgive all women for how they have treated you as a man. What did you forgive? What did you learn about yourself?

LOVE NOTE TO MYSELF

I forgive all beings, including myself, for all actions taken in unawareness that we are one. I celebrate the gift of grace—to be awake in the present moment.

●

LESSON 15: FROM ASSUMING TO LISTENING

There are men who would quickly love each other if once they were to speak to each other; for when they spoke they would discover that their souls had only been separated by phantoms and diabolic delusions.
—Ernest Hello

Human communication is complicated at best. How many of us have been in a situation where someone said to us, "I never told yo that!" or, "I said that, but that's not what I meant." When someone is speaking to us, we take their words and filter them through our personal beliefs. Then we draw a conclusion, believing we understood the other person yet possibly never truly sharing meaning.

To confuse issues further, we know that people don't always say what they mean out of fear of hurting someone's feelings or out of fear of judgment or retribution. They may say something that is not what they mean, figuring we will understand what their true intention is.

While we're at it, let's include the difficulty we have translating other languages, especially idioms, colloquialisms, and words that do not have an exact translation from one language to another. What's the solution?

Listening! It is not about listening to what we want to hear according to our own point of view. It's about listening to what the other person is saying from *their* point of view. The purpose of communication is shared meaning. This requires putting assumptions aside and asking for clarification if there is any doubt. A statement as simple as; "I heard you say X, Y, and Z—is that what you meant?" can make a huge difference in human communication.

It is also crucial to listen to the emotional tone of the message—the music behind the words. For example, I can say, "I love you" with love oozing from my words or say the same words with rancor and sarcasm. To truly listen requires being present and available in the moment. Have you ever noticed yourself either thinking at the same time a speaker is talking or answering or judging what has been said before they are finished speaking? Or maybe you complete their sentences out loud! If someone's speaking, focus your attention on them, not on yourself.

Listening and being present is an art. There's wisdom in this proverb: God gave us two ears and one mouth so that we can listen twice as much as we speak!

Let's forgive all beings for not paying attention when others speak, for distorting their meaning, for cutting them off, for completing their sentences, and for making assumptions about what others are saying.

PRACTICING THE LESSON

1. List the ways you sabotage effective communication; for example, interrupting to share your experience, finishing the speaker's sentence, thinking about or doing something else while listening (a common challenge in our overly connected electronic cyber-world), or saying you are available to listen when you are not.

2. You can work on enhancing your listening habits using the following suggestions:

   – If you tend to cut people off before they have finished talking, or if you complete other people's sentences, stop yourself as soon as you start taking these actions—and acknowledge yourself for noticing this behavior.

– If you often drift into your dream world when other people are speaking to you, look directly into their eyes, or focus your attention on their voice if you are not face-to-face with them. Remember to forgive yourself for not being 100 percent present and acknowledge yourself for noticing that your attention wandered.

– As soon as you have noticed that you automatically launched into your own story when someone was sharing theirs, stop immediately and allow them to speak until they are finished. Then thank them for sharing their story with you. Do not tell them your story at all. See what happens to you in your mind, body, and heart as a result of this action. Your ego-mind will usually fight to be heard, so let it protest—I promise you will not die as a result of not sharing your story, and you will have taken a positive step to tame your ego-mind of its self-importance.

3. What did you learn about yourself as a communicator?

Love Note to Myself

I forgive myself and others for all misunderstood and misinterpreted communication. I choose to actively listen to others with an open heart and mind to most effectively share meaning.

•

LESSON 16: FROM ANGER TO COMPASSION

Don't hold onto anger, hurt, or pain. They steal your
energy and keep you from love.
—Leo Buscaglia

I think of emotions as energy in motion (e-motion). There are times when our energy, and thereby our emotions, flow freely. We feel openhearted, confident, centered, happy, and at one with the world. When we experience this sense of flow, our body-mind-spirit is aligned in the present moment. We are not stewing over a past error or worried about a future problem. We are peace, we are Love, we are happiness; our hearts are open, our senses are more acute, and our spiritual eyes see beauty in all creation. This experience has many names including grace, Love, being in the flow, Nirvana, peak performance, and being in the zone, to name a few.

Why is it that more often than not, these experiences of flow are considered outside the ordinary, not part of our daily lives, and possibly only attainable through drugs which promise an altered state of consciousness? The answer is quite simple: in general, we humans have much more practice being angry, frustrated, unhappy, and moody than we have at being happy. When we are around people who are angry and annoyed, their energy is contagious. We often catch their anger and frustration, especially when we believe their story is justified and they are right to be angry. As a result, we wind up feeling as angry as they do.

Then there are times when we are critical of the emotional reactions of others and get upset with them for the way they feel. When we become frustrated with someone for their emotions, the result is two angry people!

When we accept and allow that someone's emotional response is based on their current point of view, we can have an experience of openheartedness, no matter what someone else is feeling. This does not mean we are cold and uncaring when someone is experiencing emotional pain. It simply means that we can have compassion for their suffering without making their suffering our own.

I remember a phone conversation I had with a friend whom I had not spoken with for a couple of months. After our initial hellos, I asked how she was, and she proceeded to tell me about a car accident she had been in a few weeks earlier. Her voice became more agitated as she relived the experience. Now, there was a time in my life when I would have either joined her in reliving this misery or I would have been annoyed with her for exerting so much energy on the gory details of something that was over and done. Instead, I asked, "How are you right now?" Her focus immediately changed, and we connected in the present moment. Just as the emotional energy of anger and frustration is contagious, so is the energy of unconditional Love and compassion.

What has to happen for us to be less critical and less annoyed by the emotional responses of others? We would have to be aware of the automatic judgments we make based on our rules of how we believe someone should act. For instance, are you compassionate and comforting to a friend who is lost in a web of emotional turmoil yet annoyed at your partner for their similar emotional pattern when suffering? Do you feel personally wounded by the emotional outbursts of your children yet accepting and understanding when a friend's child is having a tantrum? What is it that makes one situation acceptable and another a source of pain and suffering for you?

When we can see that someone's emotional reactions are a reflection of their suffering, sense of isolation, victimization, and unmet expectations, is there any need for us to be angry at and critical of them? When we remember that someone else's emotional response is about them and not about us, even if they are spewing words of blame in our direction, we have the freedom to choose to not take their misery personally.

When someone is in the midst of an emotional outburst, it is through our compassionate connection with them that the opportunity of illuminating their self-defeating beliefs becomes possible. This is the healing power of Love.

When I notice someone else's emotional reactions, I connect with my heart and offer Love. If it is appropriate, I hug them, ask how I might help, and silently say a prayer for their highest good. At other times, I simply leave them alone. If they're disrespectful toward me, I can leave while in my heart wishing them well. I trust you can do the same.

PRACTICING THE LESSON

1. Identify someone in your life who has emotional responses which annoy you and which you have criticized. Ask for their forgiveness for your judgments of them. Acknowledge to yourself that everyone is allowed to express their emotions.

2. Forgive yourself for your past judgments of other's emotional reactions. Remember your past judgments were based on your thinking at that time. With your current awareness, you can transform your critical thinking as soon as you notice it.

3. How do you know when you are making judgments? How does your body react when you are judgmental—do you feel palpitations, sweaty palms, stomach pains, anger, frustration, impatience, and anxiety, etc.?

4. How will you respond in the future when you notice you are angered by someone's emotional reactions? Consider this, when you see someone suffering, send Love their way and thank them in your mind for giving you the opportunity to practice compassion

and unconditional Love. The more our Love muscle is used, the stronger it gets.

LOVE NOTE TO MYSELF

> "I forgive because I am capable of expressing compassion. By forgiving, I release this situation from my energy field and feel clearheaded. I forgive because I can rise to my higher self and feel lighter. My light knows no boundaries when I forgive. Life feels lighter when I forgive."
>
> —Charlene Proctor

•

LESSON 17: FROM SELFISHNESS TO GENEROSITY

To generous souls every task is noble.
—Euripides

When it comes to the workings of the ego-mind, it is often difficult to discern between selfishness and generosity. There are times when a particular action may appear selfish but is generous, and times when an act that seems generous is quite selfish. How do we develop the awareness to know the difference?

The ego-mind functions in direct opposition to the spiritual self. Spirit is eternal. The ego-mind is young and impetuous with many wants and needs, not unlike a two-year-old child. It is often frightened by other people, yet it seeks the attention of others to validate its existence. It believes the world revolves around it and that whatever is happening in the world is personal.

The ego-mind never feels as though it has enough and is always seeking to complete itself with something or someone out there. In contrast, spirit is patient and at peace; it is the full expression of a healed heart and unconditional love. It does not need anything to survive, neither does it need validation or attention. It is perfect and whole. Nothing is personal to spirit, as that would imply that there is something to take personally.

Here are some examples of how these differences express themselves in our daily lives:

- When we give only to receive the accolades of others, that is selfishness, even though it looks good. The motivation for *generously* giving is an open heart and the desire to live and Love unconditionally.

- When we do anything for the approval, love, or validation of others, that is selfishness. Only the ego is capable of feeling that it is not good enough and that it needs other people outside of itself to deem itself worthy. When our ego uses people to validate itself, we end up taking actions based on fear rather than because we enjoy doing them. It is difficult to believe that we do not need validation from others when we constantly hear our internal dialogue telling us fearful things like, "I'm not good enough. I need love and approval from others. I need to have a partner, big bank account, large house, or the latest smartphone to validate my experience. I can't do anything right." All these statements are born of fear. Although they seem so very true at the moment, they are not the truth of your spiritual self.

- When we demand that our expectations must be met and that things must go the way we want, that is selfishness. Spirit expects nothing and sees the perfection in all things.

- When we feel we have nothing to give others, that is selfishness based on beliefs of lack. Living from a lack mentality rather than from the abundance of spirit makes it a challenge to be generous. When we believe we are not enough, we become stingy with our love. We do not give money, time, our gifts, or our skills.

- When we take the words and deeds of others personally, that is selfishness. People do things in life because of their beliefs, even if the situation involves us. When we take things personally, we are using the other person or situation to have something to get upset about—we are using them to fulfill our addiction to anger, drama, and fear, and this is very selfish.

- When we seek love outside ourselves because we are lonely or feel "less than," that is selfishness. People often say that we need love, but this is not true. We do not need anything. We are all divine, and divinity is complete and whole. If there is anything we truly need, it is to express spirit moving through us, and the only way to do this is to Love unconditionally, starting with ourselves.

The key to a healed heart is learning to live from your spiritual self rather than from the ego-mind. The wounded ego-mind compels us to act in ways that are hurtful to ourselves and others. At the same time, we are compelled by spirit moving through us to express unconditional Love. At any moment, one force will prevail. This is why humans can be so beautiful, Loving, and generous in one moment and mean, hurtful, and selfish in the next. It is up to each of us to make a conscious choice to live either from the selfishness of our ego-mind or the generosity of Spirit. This Native American proverb expresses this idea beautifully:

A grandfather talking to his young grandson tells the boy he has two wolves inside of him struggling with each other. The first is the wolf of peace, love, and kindness. The other wolf is fear, greed, and hatred. "Which wolf will win, grandfather?" asks the young boy. "Whichever one you feed," is the reply.

PRACTICING THE LESSON

Notice how you interact with people. Do you engage in any of the behaviors listed below? If you do, forgive yourself in the moment, and do your best to have a new thought and to practice new behaviors. Remember, these are challenging aspects of ourselves to examine. Make sure that you do so with kindness, forgiveness, and compassion for yourself.

1. Do you only express your love to those with whom you approve or who you know? If this is true, what do you believe is causing you to withhold your love from others?

2. Are you only kind when you know you will be noticed or acknowledged? If so, where do you believe this behavior stems from?

3. Are there things that you do not want to do but do anyway because you want the approval of others? If yes, what are you afraid will happen if you say, "No?"

4. If you do not receive a compliment or appreciation for something you have done, do you complain? Do you believe that you should receive kudos if you are kind and helpful? If so, why?

5. Do you manipulate others to get things you believe you need or want rather than just asking for them directly? If you did ask for something directly, what do you believe people would think of you?

6. Do you feel like people are trying to drain you of your time and energy, and do you become defensive or irritated as a result? Is it true that people can drain you of anything—or is it closer to the truth to say that you are allowing people to have that impact on you? What can you do to honor your energy and eliminate your defensiveness?

7. Do you often buy things to make yourself look better in the eyes of others? Does this behavior work for you? If not, what changes do you want to make?

LOVE NOTE TO MYSELF

I forgive myself for believing my ego-mind and denying myself the opportunity to embody unconditional Love, generosity, and joy. I easily allow G-d, spirit, and the Loving Energy of the Universe to guide my heart and direct my mind.

AFTERWORD

June 18, 2018, Lee, MA

It's now thirteen months since my romantic relationship with Beau abruptly ended. As I get ready to send this manuscript off to the publisher, I am amazed by the vast territory I have traveled in my inner and outer world this year. As much as there were many, many moments that I wished my life had followed the dream of Asia with Beau in 2018, I am most grateful that my heart has remained opened.

I know without a doubt that Love/G-d is my Source-Supply-Support, and I rest more deeply in knowing that wounds of my recent and distant past are no longer in the driver's seat of my Life.

I also know that a healed heart is the greatest gift each of us has to give to a world that is screaming out for Love…and I am looking forward to sharing additional thoughts with you about forgiving God, religion, politics, money, the environment, racism, and all the other -isms that perpetuate brokenheartedness. So join me on my blog (https://www.susynreeve.com/blog), not only to read and listen to my Heart Healing Wisdom but to share your own as well. And of course, I'm sure I will have many more stories to share as my Love story continues to unfold.

The answer to the question I asked oh so many years ago, *What would the world be like if everyone loved themselves?* is quite clear—it would be Loving.

Join me for my Monthly Heart Healing Circle
Learn more at https://susynreeve.com/coaching-circle

ACKNOWLEDGMENTS

My heart is happy as I express my openhearted, wholehearted, Loving gratitude for the generous support, wisdom, cheerleading, and Love of my family, friends, colleagues, and strangers who have breathed life into this work of art.

My first thank you is to Sheri Rosenthal, who in 2006 was my partner in creating the WITH Forgiveness Project. Through this partnership, my understanding, desire, and commitment to shine the light of Love on the heart healing power of forgiveness and letting go was ignited.

Britta Booth, my dear Camp Verde friend, our monthly calls are a treat that I cherish. Your immediate "YES!" to partnering with me on our after-school middle school forgiveness project and art show, nourished my desire, and continues to deepen my commitment to the need for desire, continues to deepen my understanding of the need for forgiveness and letting go as a daily practice.

Thanks, thanks, thanks to dear friends who are the best cheerleaders in the world, many of whom opened their homes to me to get this manuscript written and were the wind beneath my wings as I navigated my heart healing. They include: Joan and Bruce Breiner, Lisa Carvill, Johanna Chase, Calla Crafts and Fred Finch, Eve Eliot, Melinda Foster, Jim Fulton, Shanti Gilbert and Tony Farzley, Mary Guarino, Donna Hadjipopov, Rikk Hansen, Sheryl Hastalis, Trina Hayes, Mark and Robin Neiman, Lynn Neidorf, Judith Noel, Hilary V. O'Donnell, Maggie Oman Shannon, Lorraine Simone, Josie Thompson and Wade Dirr, and Jane Umanoff and Bo Parsons.

Thank you, New Thought Spiritual Center of Eastern Long Island (NTSC). You feed my Spirit and support me and my messages over and over and over again, and for this my heart is happy.

I am forever indebted to the Richmond, MA, and Lenox, MA, libraries that offered me sanctuary when the distractions at my desk were too seductive for me to be able to stay on task at home.

To the Mango publishing team: your expertise, energy, support, and patience have made *Heart Healing* possible. I am forever grateful.

And to you, dear Ryan Weiss, godson of my heart, your foreword gave me the chills when you first read it to me, but it is your Presence that warms my heart, nourishes my soul, and lifts my spirits.

And finally, to B, D, & K, you broke my heart—broke it wide open to greater Love! Thank you.

APPENDIX

Create a Heart Healing Circle and use this book as its curriculum. Invite your family members, friends, and members of your church, mosque, synagogue, or spiritual community to join you. Plan to meet for ninety minutes or two hours each week. This can be done in person, on the phone, or via a video conference. (Here are some resources to explore if you choose to do an audio or video conference: www.zoom.us, www.freeteleconference.com, www.facebook.com/live.) If you lead therapy, spiritual, personal development, or coaching groups, use this book as a resource in your group.

Sample Group Meeting Format (90 minute to 2-hour session)

- Begin each group session with the Prayer for Wholehearted Living (on page 23); also end with the Prayer for Wholehearted Living, or an inspiring reading relevant to the topic.

- Identify and agree to Group Norms—some examples are:

  - Start and end on time.

  - Let someone know if you plan to miss a meeting.

  - Complete the assigned reading and exercises.

  - One person talks at a time.

  - Keep the focus on your own patterns of thought and behavior and how they contribute to or distract you from your forgiving and letting go, not on how other people should be different or are the cause of your problems.

  - Support group members by identifying their patterns of thought and behavior rather than giving advice.

- Ask for specific help when you need it.

- Have fun.

• Use the Be Here Now guided visualization to be more fully present. (A member of the group can lead this, or you can use this link to access the audio recording at http://bit.ly/HeartHealingAudio)

   - To begin, jot down all the thoughts that are cluttering your mind right now. Include chores to complete and concerns and questions you may have. As you write each item down, know that you are clearing your mind to be more fully present here and now. When your list is completed, put it aside.

   - Sit comfortably and close your eyes.

   - Focus your attention on your breath. Inhale a sense of calm and relaxation through your nose and then exhale completely through your mouth.

   - I will now count from one to five. At the count of five, experience yourself as more relaxed, more at ease, and fully present here and now.

   - One: Pay attention to your breathing while you inhale a sense of serenity and relaxation, and then exhale fully.

   - Two: If you notice any tension or tightness in your body, breathe into that part of your body. As you exhale, let the tension go.

   - Three: If thoughts enter your mind, simply notice them, and as you exhale, let them go. Continue to focus your attention on your breath—breathe in a deeper sense of calm and relaxation and exhale completely.

   - Four: Allow yourself to fully relax your body and mind.

- – Five: Experience yourself as fully relaxed and present here and now. Feel yourself fully supported by the seat beneath your body. Be aware that this physical support is a reflection of the invisible support and resources always available to you.

- – Continuing to be fully present here and now, place your hands on your heart and ask your heart, "What is my intention for today's group?" Listen to the response.

- – When your intention is clear in your mind, take a full, cleansing deep breath and open your eyes, wide awake, alert, and fully present here and now.

- At your first Heart Healing Circle gathering, have group members share why they have joined the group, focusing on the results they desire. For example: As a result of having a healed heart, I am in a new love relationship. As a result of having forgiven myself for not believing in the value of my gifts, talents, and skills, I got a raise at work. Through my participating in this Heart Healing Circle, I have transformed my relationship with money by forgiving my parents for instilling a sense of lack in me—I always have enough to share and spare. Through the unconditional support and love of this group, I have taken a more active role in local politics and courageously take actions in service of a more heart healed community and world.

- During future group meetings, go around the Circle and have each member respond to the following items:

  - – Share the most powerful Heart Healing, forgiveness, and letting go experience you had since we last met.

  - – What is your intention for today's group?

- Read the chapter or lesson you are focusing on this week aloud. One person may read it, or have each group member read a paragraph—

experiment! I highly recommend that each group member read the week's material before the group meeting.

- Identify one person in the group who will be the leader for the discussion. The leader will prepare questions that relate to the reading and may also generate a list of resources. It is empowering for everyone in the group to step into the role of leader. Here are some sample questions:

   – What is your understanding of this idea?

   – How does this idea contribute to Heart Healing and forgiveness?

   – Do you currently practice this idea? If so, how?

   – What challenges do you anticipate in practicing this idea?

   – What support do you need to practice it anyway?

- Choose the chapter or lesson for the next session. (You may decide to follow the chapters in order or to have the leader for the next week choose the chapter, or else someone can open the book to the table of contents and randomly choose a chapter or lesson.)

- Go around the Circle and have each member respond to the question, "What's your takeaway from today's group?"

- End the group with the Prayer for Wholehearted Living (page 23) or another inspirational reading/poem/song/prayer.

RESOURCES

Permissions

An exhaustive effort has been made to clear all permissions for this book. If any required acknowledgment has been omitted, it is unintentional. If notified, the publishers will be pleased to rectify any omissions in future additions.

The author gratefully acknowledges permission to use the following material:

- **Comparison—Old and New Paradigm**—used with permission by www.WantToKnow.info

- **The New Science of Forgiveness**—used with permission by Everett L. Worthington Commonwealth Professor at Virginia Commonwealth University: http://greatergood.berkeley.edu/article/item/the_new_science_of_forgiveness

- **Brenda Adelman's Story**—used with permission by www.theforgivenessproject.com

- **Lessons have been adapted and updated from WITH** *Forgiveness*—used with permission by Copyright 2006—Sheri Rosenthal and Susyn Reeve

Books

- *The Inspired Life: Unleashing Your Mind's Capacity for Joy* by Susyn Reeve with Joan Breiner

- *The Wholehearted Life: Big Changes and Greater Happiness Week by Week* by Susyn Reeve

- *The Hidden Power of the Heart: Discovering an Unlimited Source of Intelligence* by Sara Paddison

- *The Book of Forgiving* by Desmond Tutu and Mpho Tutu

- *Forgive for Good* by Frederic Luskin

- *The Forgiveness Solution: A Step by Step Process to Let It Go* by Rev. Misty Tyme

- *Judgment Detox: Release the Beliefs that Hold You Back from Living a Better Life* by Gabrielle Bernstein

- *Daring Greatly: How the Courage to Be Vulnerable Transforms the Way We Live, Love, Parent, and Lead* by Brené Brown

- *Love Warrior: A Memoir* by Glennon Doyle

- *Unshakable Self Confidence: Simple Steps on How to Live Your Life Beyond Your Fears* by Billy J. Atwell

- *Forgiveness: 21 Days to Forgive Everyone for Everything* by Iyanla Vanzant

- *Forgiveness is a Choice: A Step-by-Step Process for Resolving Anger and Restoring Hope* by Robert D. Enright

- *Radical Forgiveness: A Revolutionary Five-Stage Process to Heal Relationships, Let Go of Anger and Blame, Find Peace in Any Situation* by Colin Tipping

- *Forgiveness: The Greatest Healer of All* by Neale Donald Walsh and Gerald G. Jampolsky

- *My Father Killed My Mother and Married My Aunt: Forgiving the Unforgivable* by Brenda Adelman

- *Left to Tell: Discovering God Amidst the Rwandan Holocaust* by Immaculee Ilibagiza

- *Writing Down Your Soul: How to Activate and Listen to the Extraordinary Voice Within* by Janet Conner

- *The Four Agreements* by Don Miguel Ruiz
- *Sacred America, Sacred World* by Stephen Dinan

Audios

- How to Forgive Your Ex and Move On: https://sacredstoriesmedia.com/forgivenesssolution_ex/
- Susyn Reeve Shares Her Journey of Overcoming Rejection: https://www.livingbeyondyourfears.com/susyn-reeve-rejection-overcoming-fear/

Guided Visualizations

Discover these at: http://bit.ly/HeartHealingAudio

- Be Here Now
- Cutting the Strings of Attachment

Videos

- Father Forgives Son's Killer: https://youtu.be/813IRQoOlBY
- Emmanuel's Gift: http://bit.ly/EmmanuelsGift
- I AM: http://www.iamthedoc.com/
- Transforming Negative Thought: http://bit.ly/TransformingNegThoughts
- The Power of Vulnerability: https://www.ted.com/talks/brene_brown_on_vulnerability
- Listening to Shame: https://www.ted.com/talks/brene_brown_listening_to_shame/transcript?language=en
- Healing Your Tender Heart Meditation: https://youtu.be/Ry10fJhVhcg

Websites

- Susyn Reeve: www.SusynReeve.com
- Self-Esteem Experts: www.SelfEsteemExperts.com
- Waking Up With Ryan: www.WakingUpWithRyan.com
- Learning to Forgive: http://learningtoforgive.com/
- HeartMath Institute: www.heartmath.org
- The Forgiveness Project: www.theforgivenessproject.com
- Forgiveness and Freedom: http://www.forgivenessandfreedom.com/blog-2
- Greater Good: The Science of a Meaningful Life: http://greatergood.berkeley.edu/article/item/the_new_science_of_forgiveness
- The Shift Network: www.theshiftnetwork.com
- Charter for Compassion: www.charterforcompassion.org
- Become a Global Citizen: www.earthcharter.org
- Tariq Khamisa Foundation: www.tkf.org

SUSYN REEVE

Susyn Reeve's life has been informed by a question she wrote in her journal when she was fourteen years old: *What would the world be like if everyone loved themselves?* In *Heart Healing*, she shares her journey to healing her heart and life of the wounds of the past. She is a master Heart Healing coach with a wealth of experience as a corporate consultant, self-esteem expert, interfaith minister, and award-winning author. Her previous books include *The Wholehearted Life: Big Changes and Greater Happiness Week by Week* and *The Inspired Life: Unleashing Your Mind's Capacity for Joy*. As an Elder, she is committed to sharing the wisdom of her experience and being a mighty expression of Love in the world.

Stay connected with Susyn:

- Read her blog at: https://susynreeve.com/blog
- Follow her on Instagram @hearthealingwisdom
- Register for her monthly Heart Healing Circle at: https://susynreeve.com/coaching-circle